SPEAK·TRUTH·TO·POWER

COMMANDER
STEVEN HAINES
ROYAL NAVY

RUSI DEFENCE STUDIES SERIES

General Editor David Bolton, Director, Royal United Services Institute for Defence Studies

Questions on defence give rise to emotion, sometimes to the detriment of balanced judgement. Since 1831 the Royal United Services Institute for Defence Studies has been noted for its objectivity, independence and initiative, the views of its members sharpened by responsibility and experience. In continuance of the Institute's aims, the *RUSI Defence Studies Series* seeks to provide a wider understanding and better-informed debate of defence and national security issues. However, the views expressed in the books are those of the authors alone.

Published

Thomas Boyd-Carpenter
CONVENTIONAL DETERRENCE INTO THE 1990s

Sir Ewen Broadbent
THE MILITARY AND GOVERNMENT: From Macmillan to Heseltine

Richard Clutterbuck
THE FUTURE OF POLITICAL VIOLENCE: Destabilisation, Disorder and
    Terrorism

Christopher Coker
NATO, THE WARSAW PACT AND AFRICA
THE FUTURE OF THE ATLANTIC ALLIANCE
THE UNITED STATES, WESTERN EUROPE AND MILITARY
    INTERVENTION OVERSEAS (*editor*)
US MILITARY POWER IN THE 1980s

Alan G. Draper
EUROPEAN DEFENCE EQUIPMENT COLLABORATION: Britain's
    Involvement, 1957–87

Jonathan Eyal (*editor*)
THE WARSAW PACT AND THE BALKANS: Moscow's Southern Flank

John Hemsley
THE SOVIET BIOCHEMICAL THREAT TO NATO: The Neglected Issue

Michael D. Hobkirk
THE POLITICS OF DEFENCE BUDGETING: A Study of Organisation and
    Resource Allocation in the UK and USA

Michael Leifer (*editor*)
THE BALANCE OF POWER IN EAST ASIA

K. G. Robertson (*editor*)
BRITISH AND AMERICAN APPROACHES TO INTELLIGENCE

Clive Rose
CAMPAIGNS AGAINST WESTERN DEFENCE: NATO's Adversaries and Critics

James Sherr
SOVIET POWER: The Continuing Challenge

E. S. Williams
THE SOVIET MILITARY: Political Education, Training and Morale

Forthcoming

Christopher Coker
US MILITARY POWER IN THE 1990s

Marc Fielder (*editor*)
THE FUTURE OF NEUTRALISM: Austria, Finland, Sweden and Switzerland in
  Europe

John Freeman
SECURITY AND DISARMAMENT IN EUROPE: The Place of Arms Control

Michael D. Hobkirk
DEFENCE DECISIONS: A Survey of Inter-Service Rivalry
STRATEGIC CHOICES: Maritime or Land-based Forces?

Francis Tusa (*editor*)
SOVIET FOREIGN POLICY IN THE MIDDLE EAST

Series Standing Order

If you would like to receive future titles in this series as they are
published, you can make use of our standing order facility. To place a
standing order please contact your bookseller or, in case of difficulty,
write to us at the address below with your name and address and the
name of the series. Please state with which title you wish to begin your
standing order. (If you live outside the United Kingdom we may not
have the rights for your area, in which case we will forward your order
to the publisher concerned.)

Customer Services Department, Macmillan Distribution Ltd,
Houndmills, Basingstoke, Hampshire, RG21 2XS, England.

EUROPEAN DEFENCE EQUIPMENT COLLABORATION

Britain's Involvement, 1957–87

Alan G. Draper

Director, Defence Procurement Management Group
Royal Military College of Science (CIT)

Foreword by Rt Hon. Sir Geoffrey Pattie

Member of Parliament for Chertsey and Walton
...ister of State for Defence Procurement, January 1983–September 1984

M
MACMILLAN

First published 1990

Published by
THE MACMILLAN PRESS LTD
Houndmills, Basingstoke, Hampshire RG21 2XS
and London
Companies and representatives
throughout the world

Printed and bound in Great Britain at
The Camelot Press Ltd, Southampton

British Library Cataloguing in Publication Data
Draper, Alan G.
European defence equipment collaboration: Britain's
involvement.—(RUSI defence studies series).
1. Great Britain. Military equipment industries
I. Title   II. Series
338.4′7623′0941
ISBN 0–333–44817–0

To my Jackie, with much love

Contents

Acknowledgements

I acknowledge gratefully the encouragement received from Professor Richard Miller, Chairman of the School of Defence Management at the Royal Military College of Science, Shrivenham, whilst making it clear that the views expressed are entirely my own. I have also received generous help with typing from a team expertly led by Mrs Sylvia Athawes, and including Mrs Diane Gambles, Mrs Lynn Hamilton-Morris and Miss Sandra Longden.

It would be wrong to mention NATO and Ministry of Defence authorities by name – this would imply that I have received help with them over the text. My thanks go, however, to the Executive Secretariat of NATO, to the UK Delegation to NATO and to the Ministry of Defence for allowing me access to NATO records. I also acknowledge help received from Mr James Fallon in researching Ministry of Defence documents open, under the 30-year rule, for the years up to 1957.

ALAN G. DRAPER

Glossary

ACDS	Assistant Chief of the Defence Staff
AFV	Armoured fighting vehicles
AMRAAM	advanced medium-range anti-aircraft missile
APR	Armaments Planning Review
ASRAAM	advanced short-ranged anti-aircraft missile
ASR	Air Search and Rescue
ASW	anti-submarine warfare
ATF	advanced tactical fighter
AWACS	airborne warning and control system
BAC	British Aircraft Corporation
BAe	British Aerospace
BO105	light utility helicopter
BWB	*Bundesamt für Wehrtechnik und Beschaffung*
CATH	common anti-tank helicopter
CDEC	Controllerate of Defence Equipment Collaboration
CDP	Chief of Defence Procurement
CNAD	Conference of National Armaments Directors
CPS	Cardinal Points Specification
CSA	Chief Scientific Adviser
DCDS	Deputy Chief of the Defence Staff
DCP	development cost plans
DGA	*Délégation Général pour l'Armement*
DPC	Defence Production Committee
DTI	Department of Trade and Industry
EEC	European Economic Community
EFA	European fighter aircraft
EH101	Sea King replacement helicopter
EHC	European Helicopter Collaboration
EHI	European Helicopter Industries
ENAD	European National Armaments Director
EPC	Equipment Policy Committee
EPSC	Equipment Policy Sub-Committee
FH70	field howitzer, 1970
FRG	Federal Republic of Germany
GDP	government decision points
GKN	Guest, Keen & Nettlefold
HMG	Her Majesty's Government

IBM	International Business Machines
IEPG	Independent European Programme Group
IMF	International Monetary Fund
IJVC	International Joint Venture Company
IPR	Intellectual Property Rights
LDDI	less developed defence industry
LTC	Long Term Costings
LHX	US light attack helicopter
MBB	Messerschmitt Bolköw Blohm
MBT	main battle tank
MEP	Member of the European Parliament
MLRS	multiple launch rocket system
MOD (PE)	Ministry of Defence Procurement Executive
MOU	Memorandum of Understanding
MRCA	Multiple role combat aircraft (Tornado)
NAD	National Armaments Director
NADREP	NATO delegation representative for CNAD
NAMMA	NATO MRCA Development & Production Agency
NAMMO	NATO MRCA Development & Production Organisation
NAO	National Audit Office
NBMR	Nato basic military requirements
NDIC	National Defence Industries Council
NEFMA	NATO MRCA Development & Production European Fighter Management Agency
NFR90	NATO Frigate Replacement '90
NH90	Nato Helicopter '90
NIAG	NATO Industrial Advisory Group
OEST	Outline European staff target
OR	Operational Requirements
ORC	Operational Requirements Committee
PAC	Public Accounts Committee
PAPS	Periodic armaments planning system
PE	Procurement Executive
PFS	pre-feasibility study
PUS	Permanent Under Secretary of State
ROF	Royal Ordnance Factories
RUSI	Royal United Services Institute
SA330	PUMA, medium transport helicopter
SA341	Gazelle, observation/reconnaissance helicopter
SACEUR	Supreme Allied Commander Europe

SDE	statements on defence estimates
SDI	Strategic Defense Initiative
SHAPE	Supreme Headquarters Allied Powers Europe (NATO)
SP70	self-propelled gun, 1970
TONAL	Light attack helicopter
TRIGAT	Third generation anti-tank guided weapon
VCDS	Vice Chief of the Defence Staff
VSTOL	Vertical short take-off and landing
WEU	Western European Union
WH-13	Lynx anti-submarine warfare and anti-tank helicopter

Foreword

There can be no doubt that a tremendous amount of progress has
been made in recent years in terms of collaboration and the procurement of defence equipment. However, it has taken the sheer force of
economic reality to convert analysis and philosophy into actual
collaborative decisions. Even politicians have had to share in the
arduous process of educating their electorates to the necessity of
shared and reciprocal programmes in defence.

Alan Draper, in a most readable book, has skilfully highlighted the
future possibilities, in particular the need for European nations to act
together inside the Alliance. The Commission will seek to extend its
mandate in this key area. The shape of defence procurement in an era
of disarmament and constrained budgets will continue to be a
fascinating and complex subject for study.

SIR GEOFFREY PATTIE

Introduction

> There is no doubt that we cannot continue to afford expensive national developments and production programmes to produce relatively small numbers of equipments. Increasingly we must obtain new weapons systems in collaboration with other nations, to share development costs and achieve more economic production runs.
>
> (The Lord Trefgarne, Minister for Defence Procurement, in an address to a Bow Group conference on 27 May 1986)

The importance to the national economy of the defence procurement programme has been emphasised in recent years in successive statements on the defence estimates (SDE): even in 1977 it was absorbing about 7 per cent of the total British manufacturing programme, and annual defence equipment expenditure rose between 1979 and 1986 by about 40 per cent in real terms, according to SDE 1986. The number of jobs in the defence industry generated, directly or indirectly, by this 'vast and long-term undertaking' (to quote SDE 1980) has remained at about half a million over the last ten years. Within the programme, and taking up at present about 15 per cent of its budget (in 1987, a total of about £1275 million), is an area which increasingly is seen as vital to the future of the British defence effort and to the industry which supports it, namely collaboration with other countries in the development of major new defence systems.

Such collaboration, in its evolution and growth over the last thirty years, represents an international defence phenomenon to which future historians may give a significance almost on a par with the postwar spawnings of international defence organisations in terms of its military and political importance as well as its economic consequences: in both areas, results have been achieved against the odds since the Second World War, given the very great difficulties in the path of independent nations in forming multinational alliances or even co-operative arrangements for harmonising equipment requirements. The activities of multinational corporations had given an insight since the beginning of this century into the advantages to be gained from supranational collaboration, but governments, slower to

1

move, accepted only half a century later that weapons collaboration could be advantageous to defence programmes. An indication of the way forward had been given at the highest level in 1957. In defence circles, 1957 is remembered as the year of the Sandys White Paper, which initiated progress towards the centralisation of British defence – actually, it was Mr Harold Macmillan, as he then was, who should be remembered as the architect of this movement; he announced that January that the Minister of Defence would henceforth have the authority to decide on all matters affecting the armed forces, including their equipment. He was, in the following October, a signatory of the declaration of common purpose issued by President Eisenhower and himself two months before NATO Heads of Government announced measures for closer policy co-operation within the Alliance. After the lessons of Suez and the launching of the first Soviet sputnik, the declaration used the word 'interdependence' to identify the future political needs of the West. The word gained rapid currency in Whitehall, but, although equipment interdependence discussions had already begun in the NATO context, the concept found its first public expression in relation to the British defence equipment programme in SDE 1961, where, in a paragraph headed 'Interdependence', high-flying plans for the future were outlined. The text asserted that Britain had been in the lead in offering the results of research and development (R&D) efforts to NATO, and had put forward plans for accelerating progress towards interdependence by concentrating effort on a selected number of major weapons projects.These plans had been approved at the last meeting of the NATO Defence Ministers, in December 1960, and Her Majesty's Government (HMG) welcomed this decision to press on with the projects to achieve speedy results.

These references to NATO are the pointer to the location and focus of Anglo/American efforts to put flesh on the 1957 declaration. The British had presented to NATO Defence Ministers their progress plans for interdependent arms co-operation as early as April 1958: soon after, the NATO Defence Production Committee (which became the Armaments Committee) and subsequently the NATO Council itself, in November 1959, approved procedures for the implementation of future projects for research into, and development and production of modern weapons and equipment. Now that the procedural backbone had been set in place, the British once more set out, in the following year, plans for co-operation in a smaller and more realistic number of areas.

On the face of things, three years had thus elapsed without significant progress towards equipment interdependence, although the British had taken a political lead twice during that period. In fact, already in 1957 there had been real progress at sub-ministerial level with the first fully-fledged NATO defence project – 'fully-fledged' in the sense that NATO military authorities formulated operational requirements for a maritime patrol aircraft which were subsequently converted into operational characteristics by the national representatives who formed NATO's Defence Production Committee. Seven nations, including Britain, submitted design studies; the choice of the French Bréguet 1150 was announced later, and British interest at once seemed to evaporate, except in so far as Rolls-Royce and de Havilland continued to be involved in the development, the one for the engine and the other for the propellers, and subsequently profited from orders for the aircraft.

So what went wrong between 1957 and 1966, when the first analysis of the development of equipment collaboration was set out in the statement on the defence estimates? Why did not the high-flying political intentions of the Eisenhower/Macmillan declaration flower into more effective co-operation in armaments? The Plowden Committee on the Aircraft Industry commented in 1965 that 'Interdependence in aircraft development and production has been official policy for about ten years. Progress has, however, been slow. The policy will have to be given a far more powerful momentum to achieve extended collaboration within Europe in the next five to ten years.' SDE 1966 acknowledged that 'progress that is with [multilateral development] was so far disappointing' and that 'better success had been obtained with bilateral efforts', yet the needed momentum was given for more successful collaboration in major defence projects between 1966 and 1987.

A first survey of the history of the first thirty years of British involvement in this area of European collaborative procurement may be timely, even although it is an administrative and political analysis rather than a study undertaken from a military or technological perspective. Much remains to be written on collaboration in defence research, but the present survey will leave this area aside so as to focus on collaboration in what SDE 80 called 'major future weapons systems', an expression which in its context relates to conventional weapons and also excludes the Strategic Defence Initiative (SDI) as well as strategic and theatre nuclear weapons. The objectives will be threefold:

(a) to examine why early collaborative projects, as defined, in the period 1957–76 had comparatively little success;

(b) to consider the reasons for the highly significant progress made between 1976 and 1987, and to identify any major implications;

(c) and to draw on the experience of the last thirty years in considering the consequences for the nation (and particularly its defence industry) of successful equipment collaboration in Europe during the years ahead in a way which holds a balance with the advantages to be gained from equipment collaboration with the United States.

1 Stages for Collaboration

'Defence procurement' is the process of obtaining equipment for defence forces by a variety of means, which include:

(a) purchase, loan or gift;
(b) production under licence;
(c) joint development or production on another country's designs;
(d) national development and production;
(e) up-dating existing equipment;
(f) *ab initio* collaboration;
(g) arrangements for offset;
(h) agreements with one or more other countries to co-ordinate development and production programmes.

All these processes can involve 'projects', in the sense that a project is a planned equipment which is to be acquired or produced by one of these means, and most of them involve some measure of liaison with other countries. Production under licence, and joint production – alternatively known as 'co-production' or 'multinational production' – are forms of collaboration whose advantages and disadvantages are outlined, for the sake of completeness, in this chapter. The ideal form of a 'defence collaborative project' is that of an item or items of equipment discussed between two or more nations aiming at the harmonisation of operational concepts – whether this discussion takes place at NATO headquarters or, initially, in the defence headquarters of the participating countries, or between defence industrial firms. In other words, it is defence procurement through the method of *ab initio* collaboration, moving first from concepts through joint staff targets to feasibility study, staff requirements and project definition, and thence to common development and production, always with two or more nations participating. By definition, this excludes research and logistics collaboration. In describing *ab initio* collaboration as ideal, in the sense that it is a systematic and orderly approach to common requirements, my intention is not to denigrate successful collaborative ventures which sprang from political or industrial necessity or from a sudden realisation that national projects already begun could be linked, even at a late stage of development, with those of other countries.

Any new major[1] defence project begins its life after Defence Ministries realise that a new idea or new ideas are needed to meet one or more of a series of finite situations; the main possibilities are when:

(a) equipment is technologically obsolete or obsolescent, and must be replaced if it cannot be modified;

(b) the enemy, or potential enemy, has changed his technology or strategy in such a way that countermeasures must be taken by acquiring new forms of equipment;

(c) new areas of technology have been identified through defence or commercial research, which are likely to make existing systems obsolete, and thus necessitate a reassessment of future systems;

(d) a serious defect has appeared in existing equipment which compels its replacement;

(e) changes have been made in defence policy or in military strategy and/or tactics which call for new equipment.

In the British Ministry of Defence, ideas for new equipment have traditionally been translated into projects by orderly progression through a number of stages, a procedure which has been standard since the 1960s, following the report of the Downey Committee (William Downey was an Under-Secretary in the then Ministry of Aviation), which was established by the administration of the day to seek remedies for the lack of clear procedures for equipment development and control, such as had enabled certain firms to make unacceptable profits at the government's expense. The first step is 'concept formulation', covering the period between the collection of ideas and the formal statement of an operational need: as many interests as possible are consulted in a search for constructive ideas by staff in the operational requirements section of the Ministry. Those who are to use the equipment have a key input in discussions with scientists and engineers in the government service and with defence industry and the universities. Over a period of time, a 'staff target' which is a broad description of what is needed, with outline functions and performance required, is prepared and endorsed before 'feasibility study'. Defence firms (with access to or in competition with Defence Research Establishments) undertake studies to work out whether and how the target could be met and indicate in their proposals roughly how much it would cost and when equipment might be ready. The solution preferred by the Ministry is endorsed as a 'staff requirement' – a detailed statement of the function, performance, time-scale and cost of a proposed weapon system. By the time this stage is reached, a project (with its linked related projects) will have a place in the long-term costings, and there should be clear departmental ideas on whether collaboration is involved and, if so, with which countries. Equally, the technology involved, and the amount of risk, should be known, along with likely contractors and the export potential.

The vital next stage is 'project definition', in which firms once more compete to prepare a detailed plan for the development of a system, with the aim of eliminating or reducing areas of risk: the Downey Report identified the preparation of such a plan as the key to entering 'full development' and as the major output to be expected from 'feasibility study' and 'project definition'. This 'development cost plan' gives details of costs, time and resources estimated to be necessary, and the arrangements for project management and control to be employed; 'project definition' is, for any major project, a necessary prelude to ministerial approval of the costly 'development' stage, when detailed specifications take material form. Before approving development, ministers are made aware of production plans for the system, and implications for employment and sales: in the past, production has often begun before development ended. Changes in defence contract procedures introduced in 1986 have made it less automatic for production contracts to go to the contractor charged with development, who in earlier years was almost guaranteed production orders, but may now have to compete for production.

A new approach to major equipment has emerged in recent years and now runs in parallel with the more formal Downey procedures. The cardinal points specification procedures were first used by the Navy Department of the Ministry of Defence; under the procedures, the military authorities responsible for concept identification specify in terms of performance the 'cardinal points' of planned equipment 'which define key performance features, but otherwise allow industry the maximum scope to innovate, cut costs and enhance the export potential of the equipment' (SDE 86). The procedures are especially useful where defence and civil interests converge in the same broad area of advanced technology.

In the early days of collaboration, ideas differed markedly on the stage at which collaboration could most usefully begin. For example, in January 1977, the Political Affairs Committee of the European Parliament invited Dr Egon Klepsch, a German MEP with extensive experience of Western European Union (WEU), the Council of Europe and the North Atlantic Assembly, to report on action which the Parliament might take to improve co-operation in European defence procurement. Dr Klepsch's report, made to the Parliament's Political Committee in the same year, and endorsed by the European Parliament in 1978, recommended *inter alia* that the European Commission should make proposals for EEC financing of collaborative European procurement policies, including defence procurement. Although this idea has not borne fruit, the report itself, published as *Two-way Street*,[2] contains much useful material on collaboration as seen in the mid-1970s, not least in the comments included by Tom Normanton, MP, on behalf of the Parliament's Committee on Economic and Monetary Affairs. In these, Normanton identifies concisely the existing major forms of co-operation between national defence procurement authorities and defence firms, with an appraisal of their advantages and disadvantages, making a division between the R&D phase and the production phase, but with the comment that any production structure must be decided at the R&D stage.

The R&D phase was seen by him as the responsibility of one firm, as project leader, with two forms of collaboration as the theoretical basis: (a) when government planning or financing does not take place, that is, 'private venture' co-operation in R&D between European firms; and (b) when R&D is planned in co-operation with governments and financed wholly or in part by governments. (In practice, this theoretical basis was not found appropriate to early collaborative ventures, as early government involvement was crucial.) The limits of co-operation were seen as restricted by the need to match the R&D phase with the production facilities available; if new production partners had to be found, and their alterations to the project incorporated, there would be delays and cost increases. The forms of co-operation identified were:

(a)   internationally-divided labour allocation to national production geared to national needs; most experts have seen this as a pipe-dream, despite its theoretical advantages, and it can be disregarded as implying a degree of international interdependence, and a willingness to sacrifice the interest of national defence industries, ends which are unlikely to be realised in the present century;

(b) production under licence;
(c) co-production.

Three main advantages of co-production were identified in *Two-way Street*. The first is that such collaboration enables participating countries to move into technological areas formerly beyond their national reach, with some spin-off both for the national defence industry itself and for the engineers and scientists who are involved with the project. Additionally, the individual national requirements of several partners can be met by this method, so it carries significant advantages of flexibility over production under licence, and should result in lower unit costs than national production. Finally, firms involved with co-production can spread the advantages to their sub-contractors.

Many international collaborative programmes have involved either production under licence or a form of co-production using a design developed by a participating or a non-participating nation, in which case either a licence is bought or a contribution paid to the developer's costs. In fact, the first NATO multinational project, beginning in 1954, for a lightweight tactical reconnaissance aircraft, resulted in the production in the Federal Republic of Germany (FRG) of the Italian G91. Since then, many weapon systems of American design have been co-produced by NATO member countries, the most notable in NATO's early years being the Hawk and the Sidewinder programmes.

After thirty years' experience of co-production, participating nations have refined and expanded the original methodology so as to maximise advantages. A topical example is the multiple-launch rocket system (MLRS), which was due to begin European production in 1987 on the basis of an American-developed system: participating countries are Britain, France, the FRG and Italy, with Italy dropping out of phase two, which is under development. Each country's logistic authorities have been able to plan in advance detailed arrangements for the European deployment of the system. Additionally, the five national industrial firms involved (including the Americans) have formed a joint company to market the system when produced. It is reasonable to assume that over half of NATO'S European members will have this system deployed on their territory, either as producers or as customers, by the end of the 1990s. The huge members of systems resulting from NATO deployment, added to global sales, bring obvious strategic and economical advantages to the sections of the national defence industry involved, as well as providing NATO with the military advantages of standardisation and interoperability.

Nevertheless co-production has limitations as a form of collaboration which make it second-best in many cases to *ab initio* collaboration. There is bound to be the risk that the technology used will be quickly outdated, if it is based on elderly designs. There is also the risk that countries will be tempted to take on ambitious production capacities which are beyond their national economic capacity to sustain. And there is the financial risk that premiums to be paid, added to production costs, mean that, in the end, much more will have been paid out per unit than if the equipment had been bought off the shelf. Co-production can be successful if one system with universal application (like the MLRS) is involved, and it is applicable if one nation (such as the United States) is so technologically advanced that its partners are almost obliged to use this method to achieve their ends. It was the second of these factors which led to the concern expressed by Normanton after his analysis of collaborative methods that

> unless action is taken at an early date to lay down on a joint basis the military requirements for the equipment in question, and this is followed up by cooperation on the manufacture and procurement of standardised material, it is to be feared that the most competitive European undertakings will enter into collaboration on production with American companies, and that the remaining firms will disappear from the market.

Equally, the Rt Hon. Geoffrey Rippon, MP, in his foreword to *Two-way Street*, commented that 'although the United States can organise American firms to meet the equipment needs of a homogeneous market, absence of action by the European Community will force increasing technological dependence by European firms on the know-how of the United States'. A major advantage provided by *ab initio* collaboration, and which is missing from co-production, is that it gives European firms, through association with the development of concepts, the opportunity to compete for design leadership of a project, thus retaining in Europe the capability to retain, develop and employ the skills of designers, which, along with cost-effective management, are the basic requirements for enabling European firms to compete successfully in the defence market with American firms. On the other hand, the method demands long and careful preparation to harmonise military requirements and time-scales.

In the early days of British involvement in collaboration with countries in Western Europe in the procurement of weapons systems, it was convenient to accept that British firms should produce to other countries' designs. For example, as Britain's influence as a world power declined steadily between 1958 and 1966, it was almost inevitable that this country should have relied heavily on development work in the United States in equipping the British armed forces; additionally, in these years, political factors led to the cancellation of 32 major nationally-planned weapon systems, including Blue Streak and the TSR 2, at a cost, at the value of those years, of £500 million. Likewise, as Britain turned towards collaboration with Europe, it was acceptable to reach agreements (such as the Anglo-French helicopter deal described in Chapter 8) whereby a British firm put together components, or produced systems, which had been designed and developed elsewhere. By the mid-1970s, however, although the national economy in other areas was in trouble, the proportion of the defence budget devoted to equipment increased strikingly by comparison with other European countries (see Table 1.1), and even topped the comparable percentage in the United States in the decade

TABLE 1.1 *Percentage of national defence budgets for equipment, 1970–87 (NATO figures and conventions)*

Country	Average 1970–4	Average 1975–9	Average 1980–4	1980	1983	1984	1985	1986	1987
Belgium	10.7	11.7	13.8	14.4	13.8	13.2	12.7	12.9	12.7
Canada	7.3	9.0	17.8	15.4	20.4	20.8	18.5	20.2	19.0
Denmark	16.4	18.4	16.9	18.1	16.5	15.7	13.8	14.0	16.3
Germany	11.9	12.8	16.6	14.8	17.3	16.5	14.8	15.9	15.5
Greece	8.2	19.3	17.4	18.8	15.9	15.3	14.5	15.8	18.6
Italy	15.3	14.7	17.4	17.5	18.5	17.3	18.8	18.4	17.8
Luxembourg	1.5	1.9	1.8	1.8	1.7	1.6	4.0	3.1	4.2
Netherlands	12.8	18.0	20.5	18.0	22.9	23.2	23.4	20.3	20.1
Norway	15.2	16.0	19.4	19.3	21.1	18.1	24.9	20.2	21.1
Portugal	7.1	2.2	5.5	6.1	4.9	4.8	3.3	6.3	11.6
Turkey	3.9	19.2	9.1	4.7	10.1	13.1	13.6	17.9	21.1
United Kingdom	16.6	21.6	26.2	25.2	26.7	27.2	27.0	25.2	26.2
United States	21.4	17.6	21.9	19.5	23.5	25.2	25.7	25.8	27.1

1975–85. This change of emphasis gave British designers (both in government establishments and in the defence industry) the means and the confidence at least to match the efforts of their colleagues in other countries, with the result that Britain achieved a position which has not been lost in taking the lead in the inception of collaborative projects.

The background in NATO to the emergence of fuller British involvement in collaborative projects will be described in the next chapter. As to the lessons learned during the period under review on the stages of the procurement process most appropriate for collaboration, a prime factor to have emerged is that collaboration is likely to produce the greatest financial savings for governments through sharing the high costs foreseen for major projects at the development stage. A prerequisite for entry into development, as we have seen, is that earlier phases should have been carried out with meticulous thoroughness: there are also strong arguments for testing the planned design through initial demonstrations of hardware before a decision is taken to begin development. The advantages of collaboration at the production stage have become increasingly dubious, and any NATO government planning on co-production as a form of collaboration will be well advised to consider very carefully whether the premium to be paid is really justified in terms of overall national economic considerations. Certainly NATO Ministers of Defence have placed increasing emphasis on the planned co-ordination of operational requirements as a prelude to collaboration.

If, then, collaboration is to be commended as a method of sharing development costs, only two approaches are really valid. One is the *ab initio* approach, through harmonisation of requirements. The other is the identification by one or more nations of items already under way in another nation's development programme which come close enough to their needs to enable collaboration to be agreed in sharing developments. Clearly the second method will be more attractive to the nation with the development programme if some *quid pro quo* is available in the form of an interesting development item in the catalogue of development items of the other countries. Thus it is a method of appeal mainly to NATO countries with advanced technological programmes.

2 The NATO Background: 1957 to 1976

In trying to understand why successive British governments took no decisive steps towards collaboration in European equipment programmes for almost ten years following the 1957 declaration, a brief analysis of the political and organisational background in NATO during those years is needed, as it gives part of the explanation. A Defence Production Board came into existence early in NATO's history with the aims of helping to increase production in member countries and of facilitating joint use of industrial installations – even before the NATO Council itself had been instituted and NATO had become a permanent organisation. Initially the task of improving national defence equipment programmes was undertaken through help by the stronger nations to the weaker, but, once a NATO international staff had been established in this same year, military and civilian effort moved increasingly into the preparation of standardisation agreements. These represented early attempts to influence military thinking in the direction of harmonising requirements before national production began, and the policy was thus a useful first step towards equipment collaboration.

Standardisation work – whether documentary, procedural or equipment-related – is by its nature routine, painstaking and tedious. Before NATO involvement, the British, Canadian and American military had devoted much time and effort to tripartite planning of equipment standardisation; a paper prepared for the UK Chiefs of Staffs in April 1950[1] accepted that progress had been slow, with no spectacular results, but judged that 'it is a long-term process and the progress made is sufficient to prove the value of the scheme'. Extension of tripartite work to other NATO countries was viewed, in the same paper (prepared as a UK brief for UK/US discussion before a working group with French membership met to consider whether and how standardisation work should be undertaken in NATO), without enthusiasm: 'Pressure to incorporate other nations into the tripartite machinery should be resisted, as it would lead to delays . . . To achieve standardisation, full and frank exchange of information is required. For reasons of security, no such complete exchange can take place.' Presumably the American approach was more positive, leading to the subsequent establishment in London, in 1951, of NATO's Military Agency for Standardisation, an agency which, now based in Brussels, remains an important advisory group to NATO's Military Committee. Even in the 1950 paper quoted, equipment commonality was seen as a desirable aim – 'the field is so vast that sharing of the workload is to the general benefit, and should be attempted where security allows' – yet, over thirty years later, *NATO Facts and Figures*[2] comments that standardisation, interpreted as genuine equipment commonality, is a difficult goal to achieve in an Alliance of sovereign nations.

These references to security are worth keeping in mind in surveying the slow growth of European collaboration in the 1950s and 1960s. Distrust of French security made the tripartite countries reluctant in the mid-1950s to share R&D information with France; for example, Britain accepted an American firing device for the 30mm Aden gun despite an agreement to carry out a reciprocal study with France – American security objections were the reason for the exclusion of France. Similarly, the FRG was not able to gain access to information classified as secret until as late as 1955, after accession to NATO. American and British positions shifted once the French administration stabilised with M. De Gaulle's rise to power in 1958, and as the FRG's authority within the Alliance increased. Yet the atmosphere of mutual suspicion cannot have been conducive to serious study of collaboration, and was in line with the wider foreign policy/defence background up to, and in the three years after, the Suez operation, with Britain giving the United States top priority, France looking askance at Anglo-Saxon cohesion, and most Western European countries distrusting Germany. Professor Urwin has summarised the situation: 'The opening of the 1960's did not seem auspicious for the Western Alliance.'[3] Documents now available under the 30 year rule provide evidence that security was only one of a number of factors which made the Ministry of Defence sceptical over the future of equipment standardisation. The existence of trade secrets, patent rights, military traditions, the cost of scrapping existing equipment, and the desirability of a self-supporting defence industry were all seen as reasons why it would always be difficult to achieve much standardisation within NATO. Foreign Office officials were more interested in the United States than in Europe in the years 1955–60[4] and there is little evidence that the Treasury saw advantages in European co-operation before Sir Frank Lee became Permanent Secretary in 1960.

Against this background, the development of the Bréguet Atlantique as a NATO project between 1957 and 1958 seemed, at the time, a significant NATO accomplishment and a triumph for the French, especially as it was not until November 1959 that the NATO Council approved procedures for the implementation of projects for research into, and the development and production of, weapons and equipment. What J.W.R. Taylor calls 'one of the most amazing production programmes in aviation history'[5] resulted in the first prototype flying two years after the aircraft was ordered in 1959, bearing the NATO label as a maritime patrol aircraft; in spite of this, large orders from NATO did not materialise outside France, the FRG and Italy, and French disappointment was expressed by their Minister of Defence.[6] No follow-on programme was contemplated, and only partial success was achieved. What did Britain gain? At least RAF representatives had taken part in the preparation of an international operational requirement. It can be argued that it was ultimately advantageous for the government not to have been directly implicated in the development of an aircraft which brought high-level expressions of disappointment. It can also be argued that the experience in collaboration gained by the French was of indirect advantage to us during the Anglo/French development of Concorde, for which design work began in 1959, and subsequently of the helicopter family and the Jaguar aircraft. Yet it is a wry comment on the European politics of the time that, while Britain was leading in political declarations in the NATO environment, France had actually pioneered the development of this early collaborative project – and the British government had not backed it!

In fairness, the timing of the Atlantique discussions could not have been worse from the British viewpoint. The defence budget was cut, in real terms, by one-third between 1953 and 1957. For Treasury officials of the day, collaboration with Europe in defence projects was an unknown quantity, and it would have been easy to argue against any Whitehall protagonists of collaboration that Britain's global military role would be jeopardised if the operational requirements of the services risked being compromised in international discussion, or that the future interests of the British defence industry might be sacrificed. The central Ministry of Defence organisation was in embryo form, without the strength to take a positive line for collaboration even if RAF contributors to the joint formulation of the

Atlantique's operational requirements had spoken in its favour. Also political support for RAF participation would have been unlikely to be forthcoming at a time when the Defence White Paper published by Mr Duncan Sandys, as he then was, in 1957 had been widely seen as threatening the future existence of the Air Force as a separate service. Throughout most of the time-scale covered by this chapter, there was no focus for the effective co-ordination of procurement in the Ministry of Defence (MOD)'s organisation.

There is no evidence of early Foreign Office awareness of the potential political advantage through equipment collaboration of moving closer to participating European countries: indeed, throughout the history of equipment collaboration, Foreign Office ministers and diplomatic staff have never played an overt role, although the diplomatic/military commercial link in overseas embassies has been a valuable partnership in liaison over collaborative projects and for the sales which they bring. Although Rolls-Royce and de Havilland had been associated with the consortium established to control the design and manufacture of the Atlantique, the defence industry as a whole was not then centrally organised either in NATO or in Britain in the way which now makes possible easy contact with the Ministry of Defence on the one hand and with NATO authorities on the other. So, on the British side, the main collaborative advantage accrued mainly to these two firms, not only commercially, but also in the early experience given to their defence engineers and scientists of working alongside European firms.

The adoption, earlier, of the British Orpheus engine for the Fiat G91 light jet fighter had led NATO to classify this aircraft's selection as a NATO aircraft in their publicity as the 'first multi-national venture for development and production'.[7] Under the definition of collaborative projects used in this book, the G91 is classified more realistically as an early example of standardisation on the design work of one member country by other member countries, such as was to take place extensively in the late 1950s and the 1960s, enabling the US government to use NATO as the market-place for American contracts rather than the forum for genuine collaborative effort. Effectively, the result of the American policy was to delay the advent of such collaboration within NATO for many years after the Atlantique programme. Both the French and the British governments were disillusioned by the results of NATO co-operative programmes, which has brought them no major industrial success and had become increasing US-based. The result by the mid-1960s was a move towards European collaboration led by the two countries meeting outside NATO and aiming to provide a counterweight to American marketing activity.

Such a judgement on American policy at the time should be read as criticism less of the Americans than of the attitudes of European NATO members against the background of the 1957 declaration, which could have been interpreted in Europe as pointing towards armaments collaboration as an area in which the principle of interdependence could be worked through so as to demonstrate European solidarity. Similar financial organisational and psychological factors had come into play in Europe to those which affected the British attitude towards participation in the Atlantique programme, which is discussed more fully below.

Like Britain, other European nations were seeking in this time-frame ways of reducing defence expenditure, and the American sales drive provided a welcome opportunity and excuse to purchase American technology already in production rather than to embark upon costly national development programmes, let alone to plunge blindly into collaborative ventures whose cost and time-scales would be extremely difficult to estimate. The temptation was strong – the United States had made more rapid progress than Europe in development and producing advanced military technology, especially through the use of microelectronics. The early 1960s were years in which many Western European countries were reviewing their global roles, as exampled by Britain's withdrawal from its strategic bases in the Middle and Far East: this was no time for attempts to compete with the Americans in developing and producing comparable systems, and in selling them at attractive prices. It seemed an economical solution to get access to American technology by purchase, thus gaining also the logistic advantages of American spares, test equipment and so on. The purchase or production in Europe of American hardware could be held up to public scrutiny as evidence that European governments were playing a firm and visible role in providing a military framework in Europe against NATO's foreseen opponents in the Warsaw Pact. The less advantageous aspect of deals with the Americans – especially as regards the effects on defence industries in Western Europe of standardisation of American weapons in terms of slow technological development and of the loss of the opportunity to undertake joint European research and development – seemed at the time less important. So President Eisenhower's offer to Europe, in December 1957, of American technical knowledge and experience as an aid to Europe's armaments industry was gratefully accepted, resulting in production programmes for the Hawk surface-air and the Sidewinder air-air missiles, in which Britain did not participate, and in significant purchases of aircraft, artillery, personnel carriers and other equipment. During the period, the British continued to meet major military requirements – tanks, warships and some missiles – by purely national developments. Three decades later the dilemma remained, as expressed by Mr Michael Heseltine in evidence to the Defence Committee when, in session 1985/86, they examined the defence implications of the future of Westland plc:

> There is practically nothing that you cannot buy cheaper from the United States . . . but it would be totally unacceptable . . . both in that you should never allow the strategic control over your essential defence requirements to be outside your hands, and . . . because the consequences in the acceleration of the brain drain, the loss of jobs, the destruction of the high technology base and the civil implications would be wholly unacceptable.

Additionally, NATO's organisation in the armaments area was not well fitted at the time (as can be seen with the advantage of hindsight) for the combined military and political pressure required to give an impetus to a European collaborative programme as an alternative to standardisation on American models. In the absence of such military and political pressure, the Atlantique programme was foredoomed to be a 'one-off', despite persistent and prolonged attempts by the French in NATO to interest their European partners in the project. To explain the point adequately, a brief description is needed of the NATO organisation for armaments co-operation between 1957 and 1966, and of the reasons why in the latter year it was significantly changed to a system more closely resembling that in operation today.

NATO's Defence Production Board, mentioned in the first paragraph of this chapter, had been established in London in 1950, in line with the arrangements of that time for holding there the early ambassadorial meetings of member countries: when NATO became a permanent organisation in Paris in 1952, international civil servants were recruited into a new Production Division. In their first two years of *ad hoc* working relationships with member countries, they recorded few co-operative successes, finding European governments reluctant to divulge their future procurement plans; at least they

initiated the exchange of information on a European basis. Unfortunately they also fostered among themselves notions that they (as
objective authorities) were intended to carry the responsibility of
making recommendations to member countries on their future programmes for equipment production, such as would improve the
Alliance's military position and enhance collective defence planning.
Such a role demanded the formation of a committee, and the
Defence Production Committee (DPC) was duly established in April
1954, with an American Assistant Secretary General for Production
and Logistics, carrying responsibility to the Secretary General, in the
chair: the appointment, then as now – although since redesignated
Defence Support, and without Logistics – was filled by a high-
ranking Defense Department official on secondment, the post being
at roughly two-star level.

Historically, Britain's permanent representative to the NATO
Council has three counsellors on his staff, two of them on loan from
the Ministry of Defence – one for defence policy and one for defence
finance. The responsibility for providing a member of the DPC fell to
the Defence Policy Counsellor. As the military organisation of
NATO was then located in Washington, he (and some of the other
Committee members) had not the advantage of direct military
advice, although some countries appointed high-ranking military
officers as their representatives on the Committee, and there were
also members of the associated International Staff who had retired
recently from high military positions.

In spite of this disadvantage, the new Committee soon initiated
studies on an ambitious theme – the maintenance of a European
production base, following a remit from the Council in 1955 to
identify the production implications for member cour: ies of military
assumptions on equipment required by Alliance plans. The subject
was to remain on the agenda for two years before it was acknowledged (after British pressure) to be misconceived, in that it was
unrealistic to seek to separate military and civilian responsibilities.
For almost half this time there was no discussion of the Council remit,
although French representatives were urging foreseen difficulties in
keeping open armaments factories unless European orders materia-
lised. Yet the Committee's report to the Council recommended
suspension of further discussion because of the uncertainty surrounding future military requirements. The outcome illustrates the difficulty of giving a relatively low-level committee terms of reference as
wide and far-reaching as had the Defence Production Committee. A

committee will often develop considerable self-importance (especially in the international area, where national rivalries and inter-competitiveness are in play), and thus feel obliged to undertake tasks arguably beyond its scope. The NATO Council remit fostered a belief among Committee members that they had the background and the authority to make recommendations on European production, at a time when military advice was remote and industrial advice – at least in any formal, co-ordinated form – was non-existent. Even more crucial was the assumption that European production could be separated (as a theme for recommendation) from the applied research and development processes which are an essential preliminary to production discussion. As the British were at the time the only Western European country to be devoting a significant percentage of military expenditure to research and development, and given that the early efforts of the international staff – who provided the organisation's continuity – were attempts to co-ordinate and correlate production efforts, this assumption is understandable. Nevertheless it was only in 1958, four years after the inaugural meeting, that the committee's terms of reference were widened to cover research and development: in the same year, the establishment of the NATO Science Committee provided a mechanism (which was not adequately used) for moving NATO thinking away from correlated production programmes towards the conceptual inputs for procurement.

The intention of these changes was to improve credibility and enhance authority, yet the fundamental error was perpetuated of continuing membership of the DPC at a relatively low level. Again, assumptions must have been along the lines that a high-powered chairman (in international staff terms) ought to be able to attract high-level interest from member nations, such as would be reflected not only in the level of attendance, but in appropriate delegation of authority to national representatives. The absence of significant progress over the next eight years in what now became known as the Armaments Committee indicates that any such notions were without foundation, and the suspicion must begin to grow either that Western European countries had then no great or serious enthusiasm for the concept of interdependence in the development of the arms and equipment needed to defend themselves, or that there was a profound misunderstanding of how to set about the business of co-operation. I prefer to believe that the vast amount of time and effort expended, and the considerable cost to governments of the salaries and travel expenses of countless officers and officials attending innumerable meetings, represented a vague wish to achieve European objectives at some future date, but also much confusion on how they could be achieved, although this is again a judgement made with the benefit of hindsight.

It was into this environment that the French had introduced, in February 1957, their suggestion for common study of a modern maritime petrol aircraft (the Atlantique), with the innovation that a study group, rather than the geographically remote military, should identify operational characteristics and expected costs. The study group, consisting of half a dozen European countries, including Britain, along with Canada, had met several times when the 1957 Eisenhower–Macmillan declaration was made. After a further year the group had reached the stage of recommending prototype development, but three members (including Britain) had decided that they were not interested. The prototype (with Rolls-Royce engines) flew in 1961 and, from 1963 onwards, France sought to identify a European market for this first NATO multinational project – 'multinational' in the sense that several countries had been interested enough to work out operational characteristics for military approval and to identify involvement of their industrial firms as sub-contractors. Despite acknowledgement that performance was good, and that costs had been contained within estimates, and although appeals were still being made in 1971 for more orders from NATO countries, in the end it was only the Federal Republic of Germany which shared production with France, and there was no internationally-initiated follow-on programme. Britain stated to NATO in 1959 that the Shackleton would be modernised so as to be kept in service until at least 1970 – a forecast which, with Shackletons still operational in 1987, was perceptive in its assumptions of the durability of the aircraft.

The Atlantique is still operated by France, the FRG, the Netherlands and Italy; by an irony of history, the Nimrod (which Britain chose in 1965 as the Shackleton replacement) was not ordered by France in 1987 in its airborne early warning role, and France and Britain ordered the American airborne warning and control system (AWACS) aircraft. Britain remains the only country to operate Nimrod in its maritime patrol role. Although the history of the Atlantique in NATO committees was profoundly unsatisfactory for France, it can now be seen to have aroused much interest in arms co-operation and to have pointed the way to at least two crucial military and political planning lessons for the co-operative future.

The first of these was the need for some form of high-level interest outside official-level NATO committees, and, in the wake of a 1958 meeting of NATO defence ministers, lists began to be assembled of possible co-operative ventures. The second was the planning of a new system for co-ordinating military requirements, which led in 1959 to the introduction of procedures for establishing NATO basic military requirements (NBMR) as the starting-point for co-operative ventures.

In the event, both these initiatives were to prove unproductive: they led to enormous administrative complexity which, coupled with the American sales drive, was to delay significantly the advent of armaments collaboration in any concrete sense. The preparation of lists led to the establishment of a proliferation of working groups at lower levels than the Armaments Committee, whose lines of communication as between the military authorities and the Armaments Committee were far from clear. The Armaments Committee's agendas for the next six years were loaded with reports from an increasing number of groups, with the inevitable result that overall objectives were blurred by a plethora of detailed information. To entrust to geographically remote military authorities the responsibility for establishing future requirements (and thus to grapple with national political and economic inhibitions against the possibility that such long-term requirements would be established) was to induce the separation of the military area from the arena of civilian input in the way that Britain had argued strongly against in 1957. The result (admitted in *NATO Facts and Figures*[8]) was that, although 49 NBMRs were produced, none resulted in the development or production of equipment. Even the identification by defence ministers in 1962 of three specific items which they thought appropriate for co-operation was to lead nowhere, because detailed study threw up no firm requirements from member nations. In the same year the Anglo–French agreement to develop Concorde was signed – perhaps another example of political enthusiasm running ahead of realistic assessments of costs, future requirements and sales prospects, yet at least a signpost to the potential for large-scale aeronautical co-operation between Britain and France.

Again we must not overlook some of the positive advantages which were being gained indirectly along the way. For example, among the three items recommended by defence ministers for study in 1962 was the vertical short take-off and landing (VSTOL) concept, which was to bear fruit in subsequent national projects, beginning with the

Harrier. Yet the embarrassing lack of progress from 1957 to 1966 meant that it was to be no surprise that the Secretary General of NATO (by then the admirable Signor Brosio of Italy) would be found sympathetic to radical reform in this area.

In the early 1960s, as the cold war intensified, high-level political pressure began to be mounted on both sides of the Atlantic in the direction of an increased European effort within NATO. Herr Strauss made his celebrated 'twin-pillar' speech in WEU in 1960, and President Kennedy expressed similar sentiments in 1962, supported by M. Spaak, who had left the post of Secretary General of NATO in 1961. The initiation of the Concorde project in 1962, and the commitment of France and the FRG to common defence in 1963, were manifestations of moves towards improved European commercial and working relationships. Yet in 1962 the US representatives in the Armaments Committee were still insisting that the NBMR system should continue, with NATO's military retaining the responsibility for identifying equipment requirements, and that the *status quo* should not be disturbed without clear evidence of adequate interest and financial support such as would justify combined programmes. In the same year, NATO defence ministers stressed their political will to collaborate, but did not seriously consider whether existing NATO machinery was appropriate to their ideas. Reform of the machinery was overdue if the political objective was to be met, and a review of armaments procedures, led by the Deputy Secretary General, was started in 1964. In the following year, the first and only British appointment was made to the post of Assistant Secretary General in the armaments area. John (later Sir John) Beith was to preside over significant changes which resulted from the Deputy Secretary General's recommendations, including the establishment of a higher-level structure for armaments co-operation to replace the unsuccessful Armaments Committee. The Conference of National Armaments Directors (CNAD) was set up in the belief that only representatives of government at the highest level could bring together in the same forum the ingredients of politics, economy and technology and ensure the addition of military guidance to these ingredients, so as to generate more rapid co-operative work: delegation representatives, meeting informally, would provide continuity. The impetus, so long absent, for initiating co-operation in equipment programmes was thus moved away from the over-complicated NBMR/Armaments Committee procedures, which were now dismantled, into a single forum in which, theoretically, a politically stronger, more realistic and more cohesive impetus could be given. Even more importantly, however, it became accepted that NATO-wide agreement on requirements was no longer necessary, and that two or more countries should be encouraged to begin developments which others might join.

The CNAD began its work in 1966, a year which was to prove important in the history of British involvement in equipment collaboration within Western Europe – ironically, in that it was also the year of France's decision to withdraw from NATO's military structure, and of the Alliance's plans to move its political and military headquarters out of France. In the previous year, American air attacks on North Vietnam heralded an escalation of military effort in that theatre, along with a gradual shift of American interest from Western Europe (and its sales prospects) to the Far East. There was now a strong movement in British defence and political circles towards showing more readiness to participate in European ventures, as one indication of British preparedness for membership of the EEC. SDE 1966 conveyed an intention to collaborate with the French on a variable geometry aircraft as 'the core of the long-term aircraft programme,'[9] and an undertaking that the decision to abandon the F111 would affect neither this project nor 'the development of a short-range strike and trainer aircraft known as the Jaguar'[10] – Anglo–French collaboration on the Jaguar had in fact begun some time before[11] but the announcement at this point formed a useful part of the government's package to demonstrate strengthening of interest. It acknowledged[12] that progress with multilateral collaborative developments had been disappointing, but claimed that bilateral arrangements had met with greater success.

This slant of emphasis in SDE 1966 also took account of the findings for the aircraft industry of the Plowden Report of December 1965[13] which, drawing a clear picture of an industry struggling with the difficulties of a small domestic market for military aircraft, recommended wholehearted co-operation with European countries so as to ensure a European industry producing aircraft which could be fully competitive with those produced in the United States. A maximum effort to harmonise military requirements with those of European allies was judged to be needed, such as would entail a readiness to sacrifice particular national military needs, and a far greater thrust than in the past behind the policy of collaboration with Europe. With SDE 1966 indicating a governmental willingness to apply that thrust, the coinciding NATO and British viewpoints seemed to be setting the stage for a new era in collaborative ventures; it can be seen equally that Anglo–French authorities, in negotiating outside NATO committees towards the Jaguar development, showed a recognition that the lessons of the delays and frustrations of the Atlantique project had been learnt.

The British chairman of the CNAD urged, from its first meeting in 1966, that there should be a study of the reasons, whether conceptual or doctrinal, which had delayed or inhibited co-operation in armaments research, development and production between member nations. It is worth noting that, at this same meeting, the new group recognised the danger that working groups could become fascinated and obsessed by technical problems, to the extent that agreements on the concepts behind these problems would be rare. Yet, in the years that followed, this pitfall again ensnared the prospects for collaboration; once more a large number of working groups was established, the time of high-level CNAD members was almost fully occupied in studying and discussing the reports of these Groups, and very little real progress was made towards actual agreement on concepts. Admittedly a great deal of the administrative work which otherwise would have impeded co-operation was cleared away by the establishment of groups of experts in such areas as industrial property (now known as intellectual property), inspection, and quality control, but, to an extent, this was to put the cart before the horse.

In September 1967 (a month after Jaguar had been accepted as a NATO project on the proposal of the French general who was still chairman of CNAD's Air Force Advisory Group, the Brussels HQ of NATO being officially opened in October) the CNAD strongly supported a report from delegation representatives (still known today as NADREPs) that a primary aim should be to improve co-operation between European defence industries. This was an important development, even though approval was heavily qualified by the requirement that industry should be kept under close surveillance by governments and only brought into the collaborative process when governments blew the whistle. An experimental advisory conference of industrial representatives was established for 1968, to consider how defence industries could help in improving inter-European co-operation, and establish whether there was an industrial perception of why so little collaborative progress had been made. Soon after this decision, the British chairman of the CNAD was succeeded by an American, and the chairmanship has since remained in American hands: it can at least be claimed that, during Europe's journey along this long road towards collaboration, the milestone of acceptance that industry had a role to play was reached while the chairmanship was in British hands for the first and only time.

Some of the findings and recommendations of this conference, as seen from a perspective twenty years later, were penetrating and valuable. There should be contact as early as possible between military and industrial representatives on programmes, to discuss, first, broad possibilities and, later, formal requirements; the defence industry should be left to work out consortia for collaborative work; major obstacles to collaboration were the desire of member governments to retain national capacities and technological advantages, together with their national tax and balance of payments positions; there should be a formal NATO group for the presentation of defence industry's ideas and interest. This last suggestion led to the rapid establishment later in 1968 of the NATO Industrial Advisory Group (NIAG), working to the CNAD, with an international secretariat and representatives from governments. A main task was to study industrial factors affecting co-operative projects, with the aim of developing practical proposals. (With hindsight, it was even at that time unrealistic to expect a separate group to bring much influence to bear on the harmonisation of requirements, although this remained as the first requirement for developing practical projects, and could be expected to facilitate industry's perennial problems with fluctuation in defence orders in relation to maintaining production lines.) So it is not surprising that, after a year of existence, NIAG were expressing uncertainty to the CNAD on the role they were expected to play! Nevertheless machinery had been established such as would allow for effective industrial contributions for co-operative action.

In the same year, 1968, the Eurogroup was established within NATO, as an informal club aimed at co-ordinating European defence efforts – yet it was to be eight years more before the Independent European Programme Group (IEPG) was instituted, with French membership, applying the same concept to armaments programmes. It would be unreasonable to be over-critical of these time delays between organisational developments which have proved crucial to the establishment of a more European attitude towards armaments programmes. The arrival of the CNAD in 1966 represented a major change from previous approaches and former prejudices: it was too soon, in 1968, when the CNAD organisation was still settling down after the 1967 move to Brussels, to imagine that the Eurogroup could realistically move into an area which the CNAD was attempting to reform and improve. Those who find progress in NATO or European organisations 'disappointingly slow' (the phrase used by Thomas Callaghan in 1980 about the work of the IEPG)[14] do not take full account of the time needed to bring what are nowadays called the 'less developed defence industry nations'[15] into unanimous agreement on new ideas, the need for unanimity being one of the corner-stones of Alliance doctrine – especially when the situation was complicated by non-participation by France in Eurogroup discussions. Equally, it is natural for an eminent American authority to reflect this disappointment, taking account of the enormous effort devoted by United States administrations over the last twenty-five years to encourage and develop a greater European interest in standardisation of weaponry and, in particular, the success achieved by President Carter in 1977 in helping to get the IEPG recognised as 'the principal forum for promoting equipment collaboration among European allies,' to quote the NATO handbook.

However, this is to leap ahead of the developments taking place in the new CNAD organisation at the time when the Eurogroup was established. Already in 1969, new collaborative projects which were to prove important to Europe – Martel, the FH70, the Anglo–French helicopters and the Multi-Role Combat Aircraft (MRCA) – were taking their place on the agenda of the Conference. As the countries involved had done much preliminary work outside the formal NATO machinery before bringing details of projects to the CNAD, it is reasonable to identify the five years between 1965 and 1970 as those in which the foundation-stones for successful inter-European arms collaboration were laid. This was a period during which, as recorded in paragraph 7 (and as is confirmed in American and European references)[16] the Americans were still mounting an intense sales drive in Western Europe and in NATO. Seen beside the political moves which led to the establishment of the Eurogroup, it is clear that, within the CNAD organisation in its early years, there took place the first significant corporate recognition of the need for Western Europe's defence ministries and industries to move closer together in response to American sales pressures. Yet all the ventures so far identified, except the MRCA, were not *ab initio* projects but involved collaboration on the basic design of one of the partners, although modifications to suit the other partner or partners were incorporated at the design stage, and the financial and operational advantages of joint development were obtained.

To summarise at this point what the CNAD organisation had achieved for collaboration by 1970 after existing for four years:

(a)   the contribution defence industries could make had been recognised and formalised in the NIAG;
(b)   four major collaborative ventures had been identified and begun bilaterally or trilaterally;
(c)   the first European resistance to the temptations of the American sales drive had been established in the CNAD forum, even though no separate organisations for European arms cooperation had been set up.

On the other hand, no *ab initio* ventures other than the MRCA had been identified, and the Anglo–French variable geometry project had been cancelled, although its swing-wing concept was to influence the design of the MRCA.[17] Also there were still strongly-held views among member nations that weapon systems were a national responsibility, and a change in national attitudes would be a prerequisite to any further significant moves forward. Most important of all, US representatives were caught between objectives which were seemingly incompatible – on the one hand, the political importance of strengthening, through European collaborative ventures, the European pillar of the Alliance, and on the other the domestic need to foster the US defence industry at a time when its importance to the US economy (in terms of exports, jobs and the balance of payments) was abundantly clear. Could an American chairman of the CNAD steer a steady course between Scylla and Charybdis during the years ahead, when American influence in the Alliance was, to an extent, declining during the Vietnam years?

In practice the route was mapped out during the 1970s, by successive declarations from Presidents Nixon and Carter in favour of stronger European action in improving armaments co-operation, with steady support from Dr Luns, who became Secretary General in 1971. Yet a perspective of the decade suggests that the potential leaders of co-operation in Europe were too distracted by their national difficulties to do more than improve procedures rather than identify realistic co-operative initiatives. Thus, in 1972, it was agreed after discussion within the Eurogroup that European national armaments directors should meet annually outside the CNAD to exchange ideas on future operational requirements in a European dimension, to begin common technological and economic studies if a common solution seemed possible and failing this, to look very carefully, before embarking on the development phase of weapons or equipment, at other NATO Europe countries' progress in the particular area, in case requirements could be met by joint development or production. Of enormous importance for the future also was the insistence from Dr Luns, when he became NATO Secretary General, with nineteen years' experience as the Dutch Minister of Foreign Affairs behind him, that the CNAD needed ministerial directions on armaments co-operation: this requirement, once met, would provide one of the keys missing for success. A major problem at the time was that the CNAD reported to Defence Ministers, coming together in the Defence Policy Committee, (whose initials DPC replaced those of the Defence Production Committee) where armaments co-operation would be one item only on heavily loaded agendas – so, apart from blessing new procedures for assisting collaborative planning, the DPC took no active part themselves in this planning. The disappointing results in material terms[18] may well be attributable to this absence of ministerial involvement, although this is not to denigrate the value of the new procedures planned and introduced. The Armaments Planning Review facilitates international examination of national replacement schedules, so as to provide for opportunities for standardisation or interoperability to be presented to member nations: the periodic armaments planning system (PAPS) identifies 'mission needs' for submission to the CNAD by nations or military authorities for examination by one of CNAD's expert groups. Yet both are 'bottom upwards' methods, perpetuating the risk mentioned earlier in this chapter that CNAD's agendas would become over-burdened with reports from technical groups, thus making it difficult for its high-level and rarely-meeting members to separate the wood of realistic co-operation from the trees of endless detail. The lack of real progress in the 1970s was largely due to a failure to follow through the message conveyed by Dr Luns, although the Independent European Programme Group, set up by the Eurogroup with French participation in 1976, had once again shown that nations were ready to provide the mechanisms for improved armaments co-operation in Europe. The supremely important factor of political will, although manifest in the declarations of intent made at the highest level in NATO during the period under examination, had not yet been brought to bear on the first stage of *ab initio* collaboration, in which concepts are identified and examined.

In retrospect, the main lesson emerging from the NATO and IEPG experience in the twenty years covered by this chapter was that, however many powerful figures, military and civilian, were bending their energies towards developing and energising collaborative ventures, all was of little avail unless political masters could be induced to interest themselves at the concept stage in potentially European projects, and British defence ministers (whether as a result of their own prejudices or of those of their advisers) were late converts to the practice of equipment collaboration. It is the defence minister, with the support of his government, who turns the ignition key – once that is done, the organised teamwork between the military, the national armaments directors and the defence industries can swing into play. The lesson will be important as collaboration becomes more of a necessity during what remains of this century. Western defence industries were, in general, not short of government money and orders during the period under review, so there was little or no pressure from the industry on ministers to involve themselves at this early stage of collaboration in the interest of future orders for their defence industries.

3 Ministry of Defence Organisation and Collaboration: 1957 to 1976

As already indicated, a cogent explanation of part of the British difficulty in moving towards equipment collaboration is that there was not much in the way of a cohesive structure in the Ministry of Defence (MOD) between 1957 and 1971 for effective co-ordination of the equipment programme. A group of international collaborative committees (Anglo–French, Anglo–German, Anglo–Italian and Anglo–Dutch and Norwegian) was established in the 1960s, and undoubtedly played a part (as did the Armaments Committee and its working groups) in establishing contacts and identifying equipment programmes for comparison. Yet there was no single, high-level focal point for collaboration as such in the Ministry. It will be convenient to review the organisational changes up to 1976 in this equipment area before returning to the developments in NATO's organisation and policy in the years after 1976. Although the changes pushed forward in 1966 by Mr Denis Healey and Lord Mountbatten (in implementation of plans approved by the previous administration) had begun to strengthen the policy-making centre and to weaken the service departments, there had been little change in the organisation for defence procurement apart from the creation of a Defence Sales Group, led by a businessman, which filled an evident gap in that organisation.

In 1957, the Ministry of Supply was acting as an agency for two of the equipment programmes of the three services, with only the Admiralty retaining the procurement responsibility it had held since the end of the First World War. Although the Army recovered the control of its procurement in 1959 the responsibility for the procurement of military aircraft passed then to the Ministry of Aviation, perpetuating a division of responsibility for military and for civil aircraft which (after temporary organisational changes between 1967

31

and 1971, involving the short-lived Ministries of Technology and Aviation Supply) still leaves today the Secretaries of State for Trade and Industry and for Defence with equivalent – but sometimes conflicting – interests in the future of the aircraft industry, with defence as the industry's major customer, and Trade and Industry with the overall Parliamentary and governmental role for its sponsorship This division of responsibility has frequently been a source of potential and actual friction between the two departments, and was identified as such by the Plowden Committee in 1965 and subsequently addressed in 1971 in the recommendations[1] of a committee established by Edward Heath, as Prime Minister, to consider how defence procurement activities could be integrated, and how the government's relationship with the defence industries concerned could be handled. The committee was led by Mr (later Lord) Rayner, who had been made available by Marks and Spencer to help with the government's aim of seeking to align more closely the organisation practices and procedures of those parts of the Ministry of Defence which carried the defence procurement responsibility, not only with each other but with the defence industry. The Rayner Report recommended the establishment of a Ministerial Aerospace Board, consisting of the two ministers in charge of defence and of industry and their representatives, to supervise collaboration between the two departments and to authorise policy, instructions and guide-lines on aerospace interests. In spite of pressure from the aerospace industry in the intervening years, the recommendation was never implemented. When the Defence Committee returned to the subject in 1981/2,[2] they were unable to identify why no action had been taken and recommended again that 'in order to achieve closer high level coordination between MOD and the Department of Industry . . . the case for appointing a Ministerial Aerospace Board be re-examined as a matter of urgency'. It will be convenient to refer again to this recommendation in Chapter 5, against the background of the organisational developments of the 1980s.

The main thrust of the Rayner Report, however, was in identifying current difficulties in procuring defence equipment at an acceptable cost and within agreed time-scales, and in proposing an organisational solution. The report pulled no punches on past failures, indicating that there had been 'no consistent policy in the method followed in the development of new weapon systems' and emphasising that 'the procurement organisation must be a single entity'. A major organisational defect was seen as the absence of a focal point in the Ministry of Defence to advise the Secretary of State on the execution of all major procurement matters and on the wider industrial, international and technological implications of defence procurement. The committee recommended that the Ministry of Aviation Supply's responsibilities should be divided between the Departments of Defence and of Industry, and that those in MOD dealing with army and navy equipment should be merged with air equipment procurers from Aviation Supply to form an integrated Procurement Executive (PE), led by the equivalent of a managing director. After the government had accepted this key recommendation, the appointment of Rayner as the PE's Chief Executive, the post now redesignated as Chief of Defence Procurement (CDP), provided the organisational focus which had hitherto been lacking, and in so doing gave one individual the responsibility for advice on collaborative programmes. Additionally – and with equally great importance for the future – the PE became the central point within the Department for contact with the defence industry.

In establishing a procurement executive, in 1971, Britain moved closer to organisational patterns already established in France and Germany. In France, the *Délégation Ministérielle de l'Armement*, now know as the *Délégation Générale pour l'Armement* (DGA), was set up in 1961, with broadly the same responsibilities for defence procurement, industrial liaison and equipment collaboration as those later given to the PE. In the Federal Republic, the *Bundesamt für Wehrtechnik und Beschaffung* (BWB) is responsible in the same way for centralised procurement, industrial liaison and collaboration, but with the disadvantage of being situated at Coblenz, distant from the controlling defence organisation in Bonn. To have moved nearer to those continental organisational patterns in itself made European collaboration that much more easy for the British. It is interesting to note in passing that the US Department of Defense has no procurement executive but leaves the planning of procurement programmes with the single services. President Reagan's first attempt to appoint a 'Czar' (Richard Godwin) to integrate policy and procedures failed when Goodwin resigned in 1986 because he had not been given the power and authority over the services which his task required. Although the post of Under Secretary of Defense Acquisition (the US word which covers the British 'procurement') remains in the Department of Defense, there is clearly a long and difficult road ahead before, in organisational terms, the Americans can obtain advantages equivalent to those of the Procurement Executive.

Although the establishment of the PE had been a major factor in removing organisational obstacles to successful equipment collaboration, recommendations in the Rayner Report aimed at providing a focus below Rayner himself within the PE for such collaboration were not followed. The Report's point was that the systems controllers (as the procurement heads of the three services were now to be designated) should not carry the responsibility for the initiatives required nationally and internationally to promote collaboration, or for the establishment of the procedures and safeguards needed for international collaborative projects. A post of policy controller was recommended to cover these and other policy areas of procurement, with a deputy responsible specifically for international matters, in close co-operation with the Department of Trade and Industry – the principal justification advanced for the post being that this international area had not been given sufficient consideration, in all its implications, in the past. These recommendations were not accepted: as a result, the Chief Executive retained the responsibility for advising ministers on collaborative projects. Additionally, although an important rationalisation of the separate service procurement empires had been achieved, that part of the Ministry's organisation with overall responsibility for identifying short-term and long-term operational requirements for equipment was not similarly rationalised. In consequence, the committee structure for the equipment programme remained in two stages reflecting the Ministry's organisation – ideas for projects being first scrutinised in a committee led by a senior service officer, which screened operational requirements, before development and production were recommended or approved by a second high-level committee, chaired by a senior Ministry scientist. The Rayner report had noted the mismatch in the procurement programme between service requirements and the resources available to carry out projects to completion and to bring equipment into service, with resultant 'successive waves of cancelled projects, reductions in planned purchases of finished equipment and delays in decisions to proceed with development programmes.'[3] Although there is no specific evidence that the two-stage committee structure, which continued for more than ten years after the PE was established, contributed to these delays in decision making, it is a reasonable assumption that the time taken in the preparation of papers and the briefing of senior officers for the two committees operating in the procurement area could have been significantly reduced by an amalgamation of the committees.

The Rayner Committee thus did not recommend on the other key part of the procurement process, as described in Chapter 1, namely the procedures for assessing and launching new projects. These procedures were well summarised in an Annex to the Plowden Committee Report of 1965,[4] which is worth reproducing at this point: for convenience, the aircraft example was used, but the procedures were identical for other projects and remained broadly unchanged throughout the 1970s. The annex reads:

The initial idea for a new aircraft may originate in various ways. The first phase is a period of informal discussions between Service staffs, scientific and financial staffs in the Ministries of Defence and Aviation, and scientists at research establishments. The Service Department then draws up a Staff Target, expressing in broad terms what the aircraft with its weapons is intended to do.

When this target has been endorsed within the Ministry of Defence, a Feasibility Study is commissioned from the industry, through the Ministry of Aviation. This study, which usually lasts a few months, is designed to determine whether and how the technical problem can be solved. It shows roughly how long the project will take to complete and what it will cost. Studies are sometimes commissioned from more than one manufacturer.

From the results of the Feasibility Study, the Service Department drafts a Staff Requirement, which is a more detailed document than the Staff Target and describes what the proposed new aircraft will do and the environment in which it is to operate, and includes the required in-service date. This requirement is submitted to the Operational Requirements Committee of the Ministry of Defence, which includes representatives of the Service Staffs and of the scientific and financial staffs of the Ministry of Defence and Ministry of Aviation. This committee examines the requirement against the background of strategic policy and availability of resources, and if satisfied that the proposal meets an essential need, without duplication, endorses the Staff Requirement.

When the requirement has been approved it is referred to another Ministry of Defence committee known as the Weapons Development Committee which examines the ways of meeting it. This committee is chaired by the Chief Scientific Adviser to the Secretary of State for Defence and includes Military, Scientific, and Financial members of the Central Staff and Service Department, together with representatives of the Ministry of Aviation. In addition, a Treasury representative attends the meetings. If appropriate, the committee considers the possibilities of purchasing foreign aircraft, of collaborating with an ally, or adapting an existing civil aircraft to meet the need.

If a new aircraft is decided upon, the committee commissions a Project Study from the selected firm. This is more detailed than the Feasbility Study, and covers a thorough examination of the scientific and technical problems involved in developing the new aircraft, together with a full development cost plan, in terms of money, manpower, and time, and an indication also of subsequent production costs. When the Project Study is completed, and this will normally take at least six months, the results are considered by the Operational Requirements Committee and the Weapons Development Committee. If, in the light of the study, it seems desirable, on technical or financial grounds, to modify or relax the requirement, the Operational Requirements Committee consider this. It is then the responsibility of the Weapons Development Committee to recommend whether development should proceed, and, in making its recommendation, this committee takes account of the alternative possibility of purchasing abroad and also has regard to the possibility of export sales if development is undertaken in this country.

When the Weapons Development Committee has recommended the launching of a major new project, it is submitted through the Chiefs of Staff to the Secretary of State for policy approval. Treasury authority is then sought for the necessary expenditure and the Secretary of State normally consults his colleagues in the Cabinet before development proceeds.

Although the committees identified were chaired by a three-star military officer (in the case of the Operational Requirements Committee (ORC) and a high-level ministry scientist (for the Weapons Development Committee, later re-named the Defence Equipment Policy Committee), both chairmen had to operate through persuasion and behind-the-scenes negotiation in seeking to allocate resources between the three services. Each service had a two-star officer with responsibility for its operational requirements, but posted into a service department and responsible to his service board. The system was thus bedevilled by inter-service rivalries and competition, as well as leading to protracted discussion – as the above extract implies. There was no imperative to give priority to collaborative projects in

1965; although, by 1980[5] 15 per cent seems to have been the normal percentage of the equipment budget given over to collaborative projects, there is no evidence that this had resulted from the establishment of collaborative priorities. In all probability, it reflected the impact of expenditure on the MRCA and other less costly collaborative projects, rather than a target percentage for future procurement. Attitudes towards collaboration of many (both service and civilian) in the MOD during the time-scale covered in this chapter were lukewarm: one possible explanation is that those occupying senior procurement positions had been significantly affected in their views of foreigners by their experience as younger men during the Second World War. It was only half-way through the time-scale in discussion that ministers began to perceive that Britain's defence efforts might no longer by sustainable to the same extent as before on a global basis, and that concentration on a European role might be inevitable. It may well be that the decision in 1978 not to join other Western European countries in procuring collectively an AWACS force for NATO use represented a lingering survival of the earlier attitudes which, added to arguments on the implications of the NATO programme for employment and technological development in Britain, swung the government away from the military and economic advantages of a programme which had convinced other Defence Ministries.

Despite the organisational improvement resulting from the Rayner reforms, the Procurement Executive attracted Parliamentary attention with the decision of the Defence Committee in 1981 to consider MOD organisation and procurement 'partly because we were aware of the doubts in industry and elsewhere about the efficiency of the Ministry in managing the defence procurement programme.'[6] The Defence Committee were advised by the defence industry[7] that there had been repeated examples of MOD's tendency to defer matters to committee decisions and to hold large and regular meetings for project management, 'especially for collaborative projects', and that the Ministry's work would be facilitated by reducing the number of committees and lowering the decision-making level. The special reference to collaboration is interesting in that, as negotiations with a collaborative partner or partners are in themselves complex and time-consuming, the failure of the government to follow the Rayner recommendations for a high-level appointment of a policy controller in the Procurement Executive with collaborative responsibilities may well have detracted from Britain's reputation as an equipment collaborator in the early 1970s, when it must have been difficult for other countries to identify in the new structure of the PE, and in the surviving collaborative committee structure, those with responsibility for pursuing collaborative ventures. Nevertheless, by the time the IEPG was set up in 1976, the overall effect of the Rayner reforms, in providing a focus for control of resources, for inter-service equipment commonality and for the installation and development of staff with a professional responsibility for equipment procurement, had been to provide a considerable advantage for Britain's collaborative future.

4 The NATO Background: 1976 to 1987

Although President Carter has been assessed by Professor Urwin[1] as 'inexperienced in foreign affairs', supplemented by the comment that his record in international relations 'was not particularly successful', his presidency is linked in NATO's collaborative history with significant policy and procedural advances. Primarily he helped to get the IEPG recognised as the principal forum for promoting equipment collaboration among European allies. In its early days it had the initial advantage, through arriving on the scene at a time when armaments co-operation was being changed into a much more systematic affair, of using the new APR and PAPS procedures, to which brief reference was made in Chapter 2. Both were aimed at raionalising the *ad hoc* co-operative efforts, which had hitherto been the norm, in ways which would bring international processes more into line with those familiar in the equipment planning undertaken by member nations.

Under the Armaments Planning Review, introduced in 1979, each CNAD member would now send plans for replacement of national equipment for examination by NATO's international staff, who would seek advice from NATO's military authorities on possibilities for standardisation or interoperability. Collective NATO advice would then be passed to member nations, who could ignore or act upon it as they wished. In itself, this was not more significant than, or different from, the procedures which had operated for twenty years in NATO, but it was later backed by a Periodic Armaments Planning System aimed more accurately than the APR at the initiation of collaboration before nations had committed themselves to specific types of military equipment. A 'mission need' – broadly equivalant to a staff target – would identify national military deficiencies which could not be solved adequately by existing equipment. These 'needs' could be identified either by nations or by NATO's military, and would then be referred to the CNAD for the detailed evaluation of potential options. The study takes place at the first of our milestones in the PAPS process called government decision points (GDP), at which potential participators decide whether to proceed and, if so, how: once this first point is passed, a pre-feasibility study (PFS) is launched. Subsequent GDPs occur after PFS, after Feasibility Study and after Project Definition, and after the fourth GDP surviving participators decide if the project is to continue to design and development and, if it is, which nations will commit themselves to it. Like the Downey Cycle, this is a logical but painfully slow process, with crucial decisions being taken every two or three years, and each GDP itself lasting possibly months while nations decide their position.

Additionally, the IEPG came into existence at a fateful stage in NATO project history: the MRCA prototype (henceforth to be styled Tornado) had successfully flown in 1974, and the Memorandum of Understanding (MOU) for the production of forty aircraft was signed by Britain, West Germany and Italy in 1976 – so the critical point had been reached in the first major West European *ab initio* project, and its organisational machinery had been used for seven years. Under the NATO Treaty, the Council can 'set up such subsidiary bodies as may be necessary': the Ottawa Agreement gave these bodies juridical personality, with the capacity to conclude contracts, to acquire and dispose of property, and to institute legal proceedings. If participating nations see the need for centralised management, the council approves a charter for a management organisation (in this case the NATO MRCA Development and Production Organisation (NAMMO)) which provides the high-level supervision of a Production and Logistics Agency (NAMMA) responsible for the recruitment of international staff for the project, with participating nations making proportional contributions to the administration of the Agency. Staff levels in NAMMA had risen to a level of about 250 by the time the production MOU was signed. An industrial organisation registered as Panavia had been formed in 1969, followed a few weeks later by the establishment of a joint company (Turbo Union) for the engine, another one (Avionica Systems Engineering) to give avionics advice to Panavia, and with the final complication of a separate gun development contract with NAMMA for Mauser. Although these arrangements now seem unnecessarily cumbrous and fraught with management interface problems, the organisations had produced aircraft results which were especially important for the public image of a project which, up to that time, was unique in the audacity of its conception: there is no evidence that it cost more than a national version would have done, and a tremendous boost was given to the British economy by the sale of Tornado to Saudi Arabia – a sale which in itself pushed British global arms exports in 1986 into second place behind the United States.

Nevertheless, like the CNAD, the IEPG made a slow start. Both groups contained high-level representatives of Ministries of Defence, meeting on average twice a year. The IEPG remained more informal, in the sense that it had no NATO/international secretariat or permanent framework. The CNAD continued under American chairmanship; the IEPG chairmanship rotated biennially. Both groups seem to have needed to be galvanised by pressure from particular individuals before progress could be made. For the CNAD, this had come especially after Presidents Nixon and Carter had supported the movement towards European grouping within NATO in an effort to improve transatlantic co-operation; this had resulted in the procedural improvements in armaments planning outlined above. Additionally, it had been possible to agree to general memoranda of understanding as a format for reciprocal procurement of defence material, transcending trade barriers; to arrangements for dual production under equitable conditions of systems developed by one NATO nation; and to what was called the 'family of weapons approach'. As the latter comes very near to *ab initio* collaboration, it is useful to consider briefly the progress made with this concept. Essentially it involves in NATO the planning under either American (that is, US/Canadian) or European leadership of different equipments linked within a family, avoiding duplication of research and development. The example given in *NATO Facts and Figures* is an air-to-air missile, for which Europe would lead in developing a new short-range version, with American leadership for a medium-range version.

Theoretically the concept gave both sides the possibility of establishing co-production, co-assembly, purchasing arrangements and exchange of data such as could give a much needed boost to the improvement of NATO's armoury of conventional weapons *vis-à-vis* that of the Warsaw Pact. In practice, although 31 possibilities were examined under the aegis of the CNAD, familiar difficulties of reconciling time-scales and specifications resulted finally in a decision to establish only one programme – by a strange coincidence, the one identified as an example in *NATO Facts and Figures*! The United States would develop a medium-range system, the advanced medium-range anti-aircraft missile (AMRAAM) and a European consortium a short-range version (ASRAAM): at the time of the CNAD's study, no new short-range system was being developed, but some European countries foresaw a need to replace the successful Sidewinder missile. The first mention of ASRAAM in the statements on the defence estimates came in 1987, with the FRG and Norway identified as Britain's partners in the development: professional journals have shown interest in the project since the memorandum of understanding was signed, and Sir Raymond Lygo was already in 1986 expressing BAe's impatience with the lack of movement on the part of the FRG. When the MOU was signed, the AMRAAM programme had already begun, with a planned in-service date of 1987, which has now slipped: the delay in the AMRAAM time-scale is an additional reason for concern for Europe in the sense that decisions to co-produce are also delayed. Finally, development of some of the aircraft which will carry the missiles has proceeded separately, with the USAF backing an advanced tactical fighter (ATF) programme, and the FRG and Britain participating with Italy and Spain in developing a European fighter aircraft (EFA). As neither aircraft had been identified when the missile programmes started, there may well be a risk of a change of design specifications such as would delay ASRAAM yet again.

So, until AMRAAM and ASRAAM are clear of these teething problems, and their value to the Alliance (and subsequently as external sales prospects) has been tested, the 'family of weapons' approach will remain an interesting but unproven venture under the control of the CNAD. Viewed from the perspective of value for money in terms of successful collaboration in equipment development, the record of the CNAD between its establishment in 1966 and 1983 cannot be said to have been distinguished. General Rogers, as Supreme Allied Commander Europe (SACEUR), pointed out to the Royal United Services Institute (RUSI) in a lecture in June 1986 that, between 1971 and 1983, European nations had collectively increased their defence spending by 27 per cent in real terms, yet he saw the lack of equitable progress in the area of armaments collaboration as a source of friction between the United States and its European partners, and commented, 'Too many resources are wasted because NATO's broad technological and industrial base is fragmented by short-sighted reluctance on the part of individual nations to collaborate with allies in acquiring improved force capabilities. We lose literally vast sums of money each year because of non-productive competition, duplication of effort and lack of co-ordination within the Alliance.'[2] Such a judgement may seem harsh against the background of the development of the MRCA and the FH70, but SACEUR was expressing forcibly sentiments put forward also by Dr Luns and by Lord Carrington, who became Secretary General in 1984, supporting from his own long ministerial experience the effort Dr Luns had made to get NATO ministers interested and involved in armaments collaboration at the earliest possible stage. Senator Nunn has recorded a personal tribute to Lord Carrington's influence in stating, 'He was a breath of fresh air. He came in with a lot of enthusiasm and energy. He was willing to take a new look at many matters.'[3]

The influence of Senator Nunn himself, especially as Chairman of the US Armed Services Committee since January 1987, has also been extremely important in the revival of the CNAD organisation. Since his active involvement in its function began in 1974, he has been the driving force behind five initiatives between 1977 and 1986 aimed at removing the blockages to collaboration to which SACEUR referred, culminating in the Nunn–Roth–Warner amendment to the US Defense Allocations Act which appropriated 200 million dollars in the 1986 financial year to be spent (in the United States) on research and development projects between the United States and one or more European nations established by formal agreements – a condition being that the partner or partners made an equitable contribution by expenditure within their own countries. An earlier initiative had, in 1984, called Europe's attention to the waste of resources through non-collaboration, and the CNAD undertook a study which led in December 1985 to NATO Defence Ministers agreeing to a new Armaments Co-operation Improvement Strategy, after the NATO Council had been briefed on the Nunn–Roth–Warner amendment. The main plank of the strategy is to look for collaborative *ab initio* solutions to common equipment requirements before moves have been made nationally to develop equipment, a stage which it was realised was too late for real collaboration. By April 1987, twelve working programmes had been identified, in ten of which Britain was involved, and rapid progress had been made in signing memoranda of understanding, thanks to the overall agreement reached on general MOU's between the United States and Europe as a result of President Carter's initiatives, covering the reciprocal procurement of defence *matériel* and the removal of trade barriers. This outcome was noted with satisfaction by a special ministerial meeting of the NATO Council held in February 1987. This 'second coming' of the CNAD had already been preceded – and perhaps instigated – by the revitalisation of the IEPG, as a result of initiatives by Jan van Houwelingen (State Secretary for Arms Procurement in the Netherlands Ministry of Defence since 1982, and chairman of the IEPG in 1984 and 1985) and by Mr Michael Heseltine, who became Secretary of State for Defence in 1983.

As recorded in Chapter 2, the IEPG, in the first eight years of its existence, had made little progress. In April 1984, van Houwelingen called for a special meeting at The Hague to consider the future of the group, and made a number of personal recommendations calling for greater co-ordination of research and development in Europe so as to lead to more collaboration. The British preparation for this meeting had evidently been careful, looking ahead to the ministerial meeting the following month, when Mr Heseltine launched his now celebrated paper advocating once more the harmonisation of requirements and time-scales, and calling for a wide range of candidate projects.[4] For starters, he put in a list of ten possible areas (following the same approach as Britain had used at the 1958 meeting of NATO defence ministers). A most important decision was that progress would be monitored at the next meeting of the IEPG in ministerial session, later arranged for November 1984 in The Hague. Subsequently, SDE 1985 registered that this first meeting at full defence minister level had duly taken place, that a number of measures to facilitate more systematic and regular co-operation had been agreed, but that their full benefits would take some years to be seen. The hope was expressed that 'a stronger and more cohesive European industry would contribute to the strength of the Alliance as a whole and enable Europe to cooperate more effectively on level terms with the United States.'[5] At the meeting in April, the IEPG gave formal recognition to a European Defence Industrial Group as their advisers on defence industrial matters. The accession of Spain to the Group (as well as to the CNAD) after Spain joined NATO in 1982 has significantly enlarged the industrial capability available for European collaboration.

The fortuitous concomitance in Brussels in 1984 and 1985 of these four dramatis personae (Lord Carrington, Senator Nunn, Mr Heseltine and Mr van Houwelingen) led to breakthroughs in both the CNAD and the IEPG organisations, as well as to new initiatives and possibilities for defence firms in Western Europe. In both organisations there had been evidence of high-level political support for future co-operation, and several areas had been identified by ministers as justifying further study of collaborative possibilities. At the 1984 ministerial meeting of the IEPG, three existing panels of officials were strengthened to supervise collaboration. Of these, Panel I, under British chairmanship, is responsible for recommending whether an area is promising enough to warrant detailed investigation by an exploratory group of experts aimed at drawing up an outline European staff target (OEST). SDE 87 recorded that thirteen OESTs had been agreed since 1985. After enough interest has been expressed by the governments or industries of two or more countries, a project group of the nations involved is set up under the overall control of Panel II, which also supervises the planning of those projects which come to the IEPG without going through the OEST stage – which have, in other words, been brought to the point of development or production outside the Panel machinery, and for which wider European interest is now envisaged. A topical example is the third-generation anti-tank guided weapon (TRIGAT), initiated by Britain, France and Germany, for which five extra partners (Belgium, Greece, Italy, the Netherlands and Spain) reached agreement to participate in the development stage. Finally, Panel III carries the responsibility for the procedural aspects of harmonisation, and carries a special role for research projects. A ministerial meeting of the IEPG held in Spain in June 1987, reaffirmed strong support for the Group 'in strengthening the European component of the Alliance through the more effective application of the resources devoted to conventional defence and through the maintenance of a healthy defence industrial and technological base in Europe'. They noted that all major aircraft projects foreseen in Europe for the next two decades are either already collaborative or are planned to be collaborative. They stressed that co-operation with North America was complementary to inter-European efforts, and that barriers to improved transatlantic collaboration must be removed. Finally, and most importantly, they emphasised the need to convert agreed requirements into 'concrete collaborative projects'. Main items for their 1988 agenda must be to review progress and to ensure that, through their surveillance of action taken on agreed staff targets, the momentum achieved in 1984 is not allowed to lose its impetus. The progress made by the Superpowers towards nuclear arms reduction has the side-effect of emphasising the advantages of greater collaboration in the West towards the development and production of conventional weapons.

The background to the breakthroughs described in this chapter was the agreement at the Defence Policy Committee meeting of ministers in December 1984 and May 1985 to improve the credibility of NATO's conventional forces by a sensible use of resources so as to avoid 'undue reliance on the early use of nuclear weapons', to quote SDE 87. Whether the rejuvenation of the IEPG was the planned forerunner of these force planning decisions, or whether the evidence of stronger will in armaments co-operation led to the plans to improve conventional defence postures, is immaterial and probably a 'chicken and egg situation.' The important factor (as emphasised by Robert Taft, the US Deputy Secretary of Defense in August 1987)[6] is that 'we now have under way an unprecedented programme of cooperative defence R&D'. The programme comes at exactly the right time for European governments and defence firms, for three reasons. The first is that no one nation can expect in future to be able to afford to maintain production lines solely for its own major defence projects. The second is that collaboration, as now regularised and controlled, will strengthen NATO in military, political and industrial terms. The third is that, increasingly, national governments are reducing their equipment programme budgets and, unless resources are pooled, serious unemployment and underemployment of national resources will be the likely future outcome: on the other hand, such pooling of national resources may in itself lead to the rationalisation, and possibly contraction, of national defence industries.

The obvious current example which brings these three factors together is the EFA, and it is appropriate to finish a chapter which records steady progress through a decade by outlining the application of Tornado lessons to the EFA project and assessing its future prospects. After preliminary work on a Staff Target, Britain, the FRG and Italy signed in 1985 the Turin Agreement for development, with Spain acceding in the following month. A NATO charter was approved in February 1987, and detailed contractual proposals were available to the four governments by the summer. After West German budgetary hesitation, development is likely to be agreed in 1988. With about 800 aircraft in prospect, and £6 billion of British orders at stake, and with all components the subject of fixed price contracts, the project is of the greatest importance both to Britain's military position and to British exports in the next decade. It has been estimated[7] that some 4000 supersonic fighters will be needed globally by the turn of the century, making this market the largest for world aerospace. The aircraft will be in direct competition with the French Rafale, expected to be in service in the mid-1990s and with the US

F18, which was already being canvassed in 1987 as an alternative, at half the expected price of the EFA, but whose technology is not as advanced as the EFA's, more than half whose cost per aircraft will be for the computers and software involved in avionics electronics systems. The EFA has been viewed as the sole European military programme which will enable Western Europe to compete with the United States.[8]

As was done for Tornado, an international agency (NEFMA) and an industrial consortium (Eurofighter) have been established and will use the NAMMA/Panavia building in Munich. An interesting feature is that, although Eurofighter is the prime contractor for the airframe, radar, avionics and armament, Eurojet, with responsibility for the engine, is also a prime contractor: this appears at variance with the lessons learned in Britain with the Nimrod experience that a project will fall between two stools if a single prime contractor is not appointed, and it will be interesting to see if the costly national consequences of this failure can be avoided at the international level. Within Eurofighter, BAe have the functional responsibility for avionics (for which no separate organisation has been established), but the cost and work distribution between the areas of the airframe, engine, engine accessories, avionics, armament and general equipment have been proposed to governments by the industrial consortia.

Although participating governments were, in general, satisfied with the Tornado experience, the cost and work share plans for EFA are an improvement on the complicated arrangements negotiated for Tornado: once development arrangements are made, there will be no change before the production stage, when all four nations will be called upon to decide firmly on the number of aircraft to be produced. Those responsible for planning MOU in the Tornado programme negotiated the important in-service stage, at which heavy costs are incurred (especially if there is inadequate pre-planning) at a late stage in the programme: at an earlier EFA stage, there has been agreement that the EFA will have an in-service MOU. Most important of all, it seems likely that, through using the more advanced procedures now available for the harmonisation of military requirements, those responsible for EFA planning have avoided the demand for national variants which were a complication of the Tornado programme.

So NATO faces up to the 1990s with a wide variety of collaborative projects and one major European venture, whose implications for the European defence industry are profound. Important lessons have been learned in the last decade, not only in the improved harmonisation of military requirements and in the use of political will at the right stages, but also in the harnessing of industry's talents in NATO's service, as, for example, indicated by the report *Towards a Stronger Europe*. Mr George Younger has recently clarified[9] that NATO, and not WEU, will be the forum for British collaborative activity, and stressed once more the need for member countries to encourage industrial competition for multinational projects in the interest of lower arms prices for governments.

5 Ministry of Defence Organisation and Collaboration: 1976 to 1987

After Lord Rayner had returned to the private sector in 1972, the Procurement Executive which he had created was allowed by successive administrations to pass into the hands of chief executives, not with an industrial background but from the armed forces and the civil service: this remained the case until, in 1985, Mr Peter Levene (now Sir Peter) exchanged the chairmanship of United Scientific Holdings for the top post in the Procurement Executive. Nevertheless, in June 1981, a reform took place in the MOD organisation which can be regarded as equal in significance to the establishment of the Procurement Executive in its importance for defence procurement management. Since the radical structural changes of 1964, ministerial representation of each armed service had continued. Although the level had dropped to Parliamentary Under Secretary, the representational nature of the roles continued, as the report of the Defence Committee 1981/2 comments, 'with all the problems of Service rivalry which that implied.'[1] Quoting again that report, 'It is the task of the defence Ministers to allocate resources between the services in accordance with defence priorities. It should therefore be the aim of the Ministerial structure to assist in the achievement of this goal.'[2] These comments are made in approval of the Prime Minister's decision in 1981 to appoint two ministers of state, one for the armed forces and one for defence procurement, each with a Parliamentary Under Secretary as deputy – a structure which survives in 1988 and will probably remain unchanged in the foreseeable future, and which, by identifying a minister with collaboration responsibility, gave a stronger political impetus to the collaboration programme. Along with an earlier decision, in 1980, to give the head of the Procurement Executive the accounting responsibility to Parliament for the equipment vote, this change constituted also a powerful strengthening of the position of the Procurement Executive, and a new impetus towards the objectives of rationalising service equipment, dividing available resources fairly between the services and obtaining the best value for the service users from those resources. It was as Minister for Defence Procurement that Sir Geoffrey (then Mr) Pattie put his signature to a document with the title *Value for Money*, published as an Open Government Document,[3] which has since had a wide circulation within the MOD and the defence industry, and can be regarded as the text for a new and more determined approach to cost control in the equipment programme.

Quotations have already been made from the Defence Committee's 1981/2 report on organisation and procurement, and it is appropriate, before considering the consequences of the Heseltine reforms for collaboration, to pay tribute to the immensely valuable preparatory work for those reforms done by the committee during its 23 meetings between July 1981 and June 1982: Mr Cransley Onslow chaired 16 of these meetings, and Sir Timothy Kitson the rest, and Mr Bernard Conlan, Mr James Dunn, Mr Bruce George, Sir John Lanford-Holt, Mr Michael Mates and Sir Patrick Wall all attended more than half the meetings. There had been an increasing crisis in the equipment programme in the twelve months before their sittings began. In August 1980, steps taken to restrain spending within available cash limits had included the postponement of new orders for equipment and the imposition of a three-month moratorium on new contracts. Yet similar problems of over-spending on 1981/2 cash limits had become apparent in the Spring of 1981, and in June of that year Sir John Nott had announced changes in the Defence Programme aimed at keeping it within allocated resources, leaving, as the Committee commented, 'clearly a doubt as to the effectiveness of MOD's control of their expenditure programme.' As the head of the Procurement Executive had been made accounting officer for the equipment vote, this comment reflected seriously on the post-holder.

When the Committee's recommendations were published, the Falklands War had just ended – General Galtieri resigned on the day after the report's publication – and the radical significance of their proposed reforms did not receive as much public attention as their subsequent enactment by Mr Heseltine and Mr Levene. Proposals from MOD to merge the two equipment committees were strongly endorsed; the Committee favoured new mechanisms for the allocation of resources and the delegation of responsibility down to project manager level; project managers should accordingly have adequate seniority and authority to allow them to deal effectively with the defence industry; the prime contractorship system was seen as affording many advantages in improving control and saving unnecessary discussion in ministry committees, and joint ventures between government and industry found favour as reducing pressure on the defence budget and giving industry a greater say in the type of equipment to be produced. Finally, although disadvantages to collaboration were identified, the committee recommended that the MOD should take every opportunity to participate in collaborative programmes, for the following reasons:

(a) the near-certainty that the project would be largely immune from cancellation;
(b) the greater funding available in the R&D stage compared with a national project, allowing for better technical advance;
(c) the advantages of a large combined market for the collaborating partners;
(d) conversely, the progressive unlikelihood that the UK market alone could support costly and advanced new equipment;
(e) the familiar advantages of standardisation and interoperability.

The advantages of prime contractorship arrangements in future collaboration were highlighted as compared with management by committee, as providing more straightforward and direct financial discipline over collaborative projects.

The timing of this report in relation to the appointment of Mr Michael Heseltine (who became Secretary of State for Defence in January 1983) could not have been bettered, in that the way to reform had been paved by an all-party consensus on the organisation of defence procurement. Although the changes in ministerial posts mentioned in the first paragraph of this chapter were of obvious importance to his restructuring, they had not altered the divisive struggle for resources between the three services, and his main aim was, through high-level changes, to create a structure which would give unified advice to ministers. Among the organisational changes announced in 1984 and brought into effect in 1985, three were of importance to the equipment programme and, directly or indirectly, to collaboration. The first was the centralisation of the responsibility for establishing and co-ordinating operational requirements through a function within the organisation rather than through a committee; the second, the establishment of a single powerful committee to see major projects through all their stages; and the third, the creation of a Controllerate of Defence Equipment Collaboration (CDEC), with its head at the same level within the organisation as the CDP.

The first of these improvements resulted from the strengthening of the posts of the Chief of the Defence Staff and of his Vice-Chief (VCDS), who was given four deputies – three military and one civilian. One of the military deputies (the Deputy Chief of the Defence Staff (DCDS) Systems) now carried the responsibility for the co-ordination of operational requirements and for defending them before the equipment committee: for this major task, he was given a joint staff of military officers and defence scientists. The civilian deputy (the Deputy Under Secretary of State (Policy)) has a main responsibility to the Permanent Under Secretary of State (PUS), representing the PUS's prerogative of advice to the military (and, of course, to ministers) on international and financial perspectives. The VCDS organisation would work closely with a civilian Office of Management and Budget, on the American model, which would match resources available (in terms of men, money and material) with military planning in preparing the long-term costings: the two groups have become known as 'the Purple Empire', and have the clear objective of ending internecine service rivalries, especially for the equipment share of defence funds proposed by the Public Expenditure Survey Committee and approved subsequently by ministers.

This excellent reform, which brought under a single, high-level officer the three groups (military, scientific and administrative) with key interests in operational requirements, was supplemented by the replacement of the previous two equipment committees by a single committee (the Equipment Policy Committee), with terms of reference covering all stages and all policy implications of the equipment programme. Its *ex officio* chairman, the Chief Scientific Adviser (CSA), is at present nominated by the Prime Minister from a university rather than from the ranks of the scientific civil service, thus providing, through his total objectivity, impartial advice to the Secretary of State for Defence on the equipment programme. In passing, it may be noted that the positioning of defence scientists in the 'purple' organisation of the DCDS (Systems) and in the CSA's staff should in time make it acceptable for the right person from their ranks to be appointed for the same reason of objectivity to the CSA post; if not, there must be some risk that the defence scientist group, already affected by financial cuts in research and by contractorisation in defence research establishments, will be seriously demoralised by their inability to fill this key position. As a result of these two changes, it should no longer be possible to point to the organisational mismatch (identified by Rayner) as a major reason for continuing problems in the equipment programme. Obviously, some problems still exist, but it would be hard to improve on the organisation as now established, which has made the British procedural route towards collaboration significantly easier.

The post-Heseltine procurement processes, which (at least on paper) are much less time-consuming than those identified in Chapter 3, are as follows. The DCDS (Systems) has five Assistant Chiefs of the Defence Staff (ACDS) who, between them, undertake (subject to the overall control of the Equipment Policy Committee (EPC) the role played by the Operational Requirements Committee in the 1960s and 1970s. The first, with the responsibility for the operational concepts which lead eventually to the inclusion of requirements in the long-term costings, is the formal point within the VCDS's area for equipment collaboration and for the British contribution to the international studies which are the starting-point for such collaboration. He and the ACDS for the specialist area of command/control, communications and information systems represent the tri-service element of DCDS(S)'s staff, each with staff officers from all three services. The remaining ACDSs, for sea systems, land systems and air systems, carry the responsibility for the preparation of individual service staff targets and staff requirements, and for working closely with the systems controllerates of the Procurement Executive, who have the task of undertaking feasibility studies once staff targets have been approved. Once a staff requirement has been approved, MOD(PE) will take the primary responsibility for seeing the emerging project through the EPC in close working relationship with DCDS's staff, who, as sponsors, retain an interest in progress until the equipment is accepted into service. Depending on the estimated amount of development and production money involved, projects may be taken at the EPC's Sub Committee (which the DCDS(S) chairs) or, if low-cost projects are involved, fall within the delegated responsibility of his ACDSs. The responsibility for the co-ordination of individual service projects falls to the ACDS (Concepts).

The third Heseltine change, the creation of the CDEC post, was implemented by the sideways move of Sir David Perry, a leading government scientist who had become CDP in 1984: cynics might comment that this move had the advantage of preparing the way for the arrival of Mr Peter Levene, but the post itself owed its origin to Mr Heseltine's strong commitment, evidenced in the actions described in Chapter 4, to the revitalisation of European and other collaboration. A major advantage was seen as being to move away from the CDP post the responsibility of being the British National Armaments Director, leaving the CDEC free to devote full attention to the work of the CNAD and of the IEPG, and emphasising to Europe and the United States that Britain was giving more importance to collaborative policy. As, however, accountability for equipment remained with the CDP, the CDEC could only provide a high-powered advisory service to the Secretary of State (like the Chief Scientific Adviser), with minimal executive responsibility. Additionally, as the Heseltine/ Levene campaign for more value for money in equipment procurement achieved more and more prominence, so the risk increased that collaboration would be seen as politically motivated rather than as having a 'value for money' base, although well-organised and managed collaborative programmes can be one way of achieving value for money. After Mr Heseltine's resignation in 1986, the skids were under the CDEC post and, with the retirement of Sir David Perry at the end of 1987, the post was abolished and the collaborative responsibility returned once more to CDP.

If this decision had not been accompanied by new collaborative initiatives, it would undoubtedly have been seen by Britain's collaborative partners as an evident move away from support for collaboration: as the British National Armament's Director (NAD), the CDP may find it difficult to give priority to CNAD and IEPG work over the other tasks of MOD(PE). The initiatives taken by Mr Younger in 1987 (and described in Chapter 10) were, from this point of time, well-timed. An important change is that collaboration is now backed by CDP's vote accountability. No European partner had a post equivalent to that of CDEC. This reform, unlike the other two described, brought only temporary advantages and may be regarded as an interesting experiment, perhaps intended as a transitional arrangement aimed at changing attitudes.

Finally, to return to the division of responsibility between the Secretaries of State for Defence and for Trade and Industry (see the second paragraph of Chapter 3), it is ironical to note that failure to move towards improved mechanisms for closer high-level co-ordination between the two ministers, as the Defence Committee had recommended, may well have been a contributing factor in the events of 1986 which led to both their resignations. Nevertheless officials from the Department of Trade and Industry (DTI) are entitled to attend meetings of the Equipment Policy Committee, and no doubt take up this right when items of vital importance to the defence industry (such as the recommendation to abandon Nimrod development) are to be discussed.

6 The Defence Industry and Collaboration: 1957 to 1987

Although British arms exports had risen rapidly in the late 1950s, there had been a fall in exports and in morale in the wake of the 1957 Defence White Paper; this (and the subsequent policy of Mr Duncan Sandys as Minister of Aviation) had had the beneficial effect of concentrating small defence firms into more competitive large groupings. The cancellations of major defence orders when the Labour administration came to power in 1964 gave yet more problems to struggling defence firms. It is thus not surprising that in the mid-1960s the relationship between the Ministry of Defence and the defence industry was very different from what it is now. As a result of excessive profits drawn from defence contracts by two firms in 1964 and 1967, an atmosphere of distrust prevailed and communications were notably poor. In the later years of the 1964–70 Labour administration, determined efforts were made to bring the two sides together to meet recommendations to the MOD from the Public Accounts Committee (PAC) that action be taken to improve the unsatisfactory contractor/customer relationship: Mr Denis Healey, as Secretary of State for Defence, took the chair in 1970 at the first meeting of a high-level body established to give both sides the opportunity of discussing major difficulties and future plans – the National Defence Industries Council, which still continues to meet at the present time. In the Council, representatives of major defence firms, as well as of the trade associations established to protect the interests of smaller firms, have an opportunity of meeting politicians and appropriate military and civilian authorities, in a way which has made the circulation of information between the two sides far easier than in the 1960s.

With these changes in attitudes, added to improvements in exports and marketing advice provided by the Head of Defence Sales,[1] the widening of the market with the establishment of new independent States, and the availability of nationally-developed products certified by British military experience, arms exports rose steadily in the late 1960s. The political and financial climate during the 1970s became especially favourable for an improved rapport between the industry and its biggest customer, in that the NATO decision taken in 1977 to increase defence expenditure by 3 per cent a year in real terms over a six-year period led to a steady annual increase in armaments expenditure. Betweeen 1979 and 1986, defence expenditure rose in real terms by 23 per cent, and there was a steady rise in the annual equipment percentage of the budget of over 12 per cent in real terms: the trend had begun earlier, as Table 1.1 makes clear, and between 1975 and 1979, the British percentage of the defence budget spent on equipment had become the highest in NATO. Yet these were the years of a harsh economic and inflationary climate in Britain, with power transferred from the users to the producers of oil, the International Monetary Fund (IMF) brought in to stabilise the pound, and unemployment at unprecedentedly high levels. The philosophy of the Procurement Executive in seeking an improved relationship with the defence industry was encapsulated by Sir Michael Cary as its Chief Executive in a lecture given to the RUSI in October, 1973:

> On the industrial side we have deliberately set out to try to create with industry, as we have tried to create with the user, a feeling that we are part of the team, that we are working with them and not against them, and that we have been setting over the traditional attitude of mind under which, if you drove a tight contract and drove your contractor into bankruptcy, it was a good thing for the taxpayer. That is a view we no longer hold. We want to work with industry.

The philosophy of both major political parties at the time was that defence firms were a strategic asset which required political protection against variations in the arms market, through both government share-holding (or even, as with Rolls-Royce, rescue measures) and orders. The establishment of the Procurement Executive in 1971, as an early reform made by the Conservative administration of 1970–4, and the appointment of an industrialist as its head, were further moves towards the strengthening of communications: high-level posts for industrial policy in the PE reflected an intention to keep in close touch with industries which were seen as essential to Britain's defence and to her collaborative programme. All these moves, however laudable, came late in time by comparison with the closer relationship between government and industry existing before 1970 in both the United States and France. Already in 1963 the US administration had established a Defense Industry Export Advisory Group in Europe,[2] providing a forum for direct discussion between US Defense representatives in Europe and their counterparts in the US Defense Industry, and supporting the powerful sales drive aimed at NATO Europe countries as a measure of both foreign and commercial policy. In France the introduction of programme laws in 1960, closely aligning industrial capacity with military requirements, linked with the use of arms exports as a key aid to the balance of payments (to the extent that France became the third largest arms-exporting country by the end of the 1960s), were indications of a closer governmental and industrial rapport than existed in Britain at the time.[3] So the 1964–70 Labour administration was responding to international comparisons as well as to domestic situations (that is, pressure from the PAC) in formalising co-ordination and improving communication between government and the defence industry.

Neither the establishment of the EEC in 1958 nor British accession to full membership in 1973 immediately affected the future prospects of the defence industry. Article 233 of the EEC Treaty specified that the production and sale of arms, munitions and war materials were excluded from the application of Common Market regulations. Although NATO and the EEC co-existed in Brussels after 1967, Article 233 was an effective barrier for ensuring that no joint policy would be attempted between the two organisations in the interest of a united European defence industrial policy. Of more significance was the tremendous rise in international investment which began in the 1960s, along with the increase in the involvement of major British defence suppliers such as Shell and BP: thus some at least among the industrial representatives sitting at meetings of the NDIC in the 1970s must be expected to have taken robust attitudes in favour of collaboration within Europe to counterbalance doubts and fears on the part of ministry representatives.

It is worth noting as a background to MOD attitudes that the closeness of the relationship between service officers in the Ministry of Defence and the industries relevant to their equipment interest has varied according to which service was involved. Until quite recently, the Army and the Royal Navy had indigenous sources for the development and production of equipment, in that the Royal Ordnance Factories and the Royal Dockyards were established within the

MOD. As the RAF have always looked outside MOD for their sources of supply and, until 1971, relied upon other ministries as agents for their equipment requirements, it is natural that RAF officers should have been relatively close to the aircraft industry.

It is also natural that the aircraft industry should have been the pioneers of collaboration during these years. The tribulations of the industry from the mid-1960s until the mid-1970s have already been adequately documents,[4] but the first ventures into collaboration in defence projects were pioneered by the aircraft industry, first through the work of Rolls-Royce and British Aircraft Corporation (BAC) – to become part of British Aerospace in the 1977 rationalisation of aerospace interests – in the Atlantique project, later by Westland in the Anglo–French helicopter package; these three firms have taken a continuing lead in Europe during the succeeding thirty years in defence aerospace collaboration. Aircraft had been an obvious starting-point for collaboration, since it is relatively easy to divide their component parts between the nations which participate. Collaboration was seen (for example, in the Plowden Report) as one solution to the industry's ailments. In fact, the close links established in these early days between, on the one hand, BAe, Aérospatiale and Messerschmitt Bolköw Blohm (MBB) and, on the other, between Rolls-Royce and Turbomeca, laid the foundations for inter-company collaboration in the European defence market during the 1970s. Equally, those sections of British, French and FRG industry connected with the development of missiles forged closer links during the same period. The establishment of the Franco-German company Euromissile out of Aérospatiale and MBB led to the procurement of anti-tank and anti-aircraft missile systems (Milan, Hot and Roland), and BAe have since been admitted as a member of the Euromissile Dynamics Group, developing a new family of anti-armour weapons: earlier, Britain and France had developed together the aircraft-borne Martel anti-ship missile.

Looked at in defence industrial terms, a major advantage of the development of the MRCA, the FH70 and the SP70 in the 1970s was the inclusion of Italy as a collaborative partner even before the 1975 helicopter MOU. In management perspectives, the move from bilateral to trilateral collaborative structures (and thence to multilateral structures) brought its own problems, which will be surveyed in Chapter 9. Nevertheless, as recorded in Chapter 1, Italy had shown a very early interest in equipment collaboration, and it was appropriate that the meeting of Chiefs of Air Staff which established the first joint working group of the MRCA project was held in Rome: the occasion marked a move by the Italian government away from the dependence on the United States which had enabled the Italians to build a strong technological base for their defence industries. The Italian government have recently voted increased sums for defence equipment to be available in the 1990s, and the strength of the Italian industrial effort makes Italy a good collaborative partner, despite the frequent collapses of her governments.

Notable omissions from this catalogue of major collaborative ventures of the 1970s are main battle tanks and warships. There is no evidence of any real pressure from the government on the defence industry to seek collaborative ventures with Europe in these areas: the FRG's Leopard I had a British gun in the same way that British firms were involved with the Atlantique project, that is, as commercial ventures rather than as a result of the ministerial interest which was a *sine qua non* of the collaboration in the other systems identified. The problems of collaboration with warship development are outlined in Chapter 7, but it is worth noting that the naval collaborative projects identified in SDE 1987 as in production or in service are limited to the Sea Gnat Decoy System, with the United States and Denmark participating, and the Paris Sonar (with France and the Netherlands), along with two UK/Australian projects.

To complete the history of major collaborative ventures of the 1970s, mention should be made of the Scorpion, one of a family of light armoured reconnaissance vehicles on a British design, of which production was also undertaken in Belgium. Even taking this into account, there was during the period a clear disparity in collaborative effort between the aerospace/missiles area and that of armoured fighting vehicles, and this must leave a presumption either of a lack of interest on the military or political side of the Ministry of Defence, or of requirements and time-scales which were so different between potential collaborative partners that no advantage was seen in bringing together appropriate defence industry firms. As Professor Freedman has indicated in a recent article,[5] successful collaboration depends upon a combination of political will and of military and commercial logic. There would have been no commercial logic in the initiation of private ventures for European collaboration with fighting vehicles in the absence of clear indications of military and political enthusiasm for their adoption. Although there might seem a *prima facie* case for looking beyond the AFV field to the prospect of collaboration on the large numbers of vehicles required for motor transport fleets, the absence of any agreed NATO logistics plan and the protection given to national motor industries were both factors weighing heavily against the likelihood of successful collaboration between European countries.

With the arrival of the Conservative administration of 1979, there was to be a distinct change of emphasis in the relationship between the government and the defence industry away from the comfortable position in which firms had found themselves in the earlier years of the decade, when cost-plus contracts were an accepted mechanism for sheltering the industry from the technological risks of defence projects, and when firms which won funded development contracts were guaranteed follow-on production orders. The money for orders was still there, but, in line with what the Treasury called in early 1981 'a matter of enlightened self-interest,'[6] the Ministry of Defence began to seek better value for that money in acquiring equipment 'of the desired quality, in the quantities required and at the time expected, in a cost-effective way.'[7] In other words, as the largest customer of the defence industry, the Ministry began to flex its muscles and, although recognising the defence industry as a national asset, to insist on the promotion of cost-consciousness and competitiveness in the industry as a *quid pro quo* for defence contracts. The cost-plus approach to contracting was to be henceforth 'very much a method of last resort'[8] – declining by 1987 to less than 10 per cent by value of all contracts – and international collaboration was seen as an arena in which government and the industry would share risks and costs. In pursuance of this policy, the Defence Open Document explained that industry would be involved in briefings and discussions by the Ministry before staff targets were drawn up and would have a dialogue with operational requirements staff on problems, objectives and constraints before any particular solution was considered. Additionally, these same staff would be encouraged to adjust military requirements within acceptable limits so as to provide more impetus for the existing policy of rendering prospective equipment more saleable abroad. Firms could then anticipate making their profits elsewhere and, it was hoped, provide the Ministry with the unit cost reductions which would result from larger production runs. These policies had strong support from the appropriate Parliamentary Committees (the Defence Committee and the Public Accounts Committee) and have been used increasingly to control the rise in defence equipment costs and to ensure that the defence budget is spent in the most cost-effective way.

Nevertheless the competition policy confronts the administration with wider policy decisions. The first, which is directly related to the second, is whether capability should be retained if firms are not competitive. The second is the problem of reconciling the policy with the parallel drive towards greater collaboration within Europe in the development and production of equipment. There are three feasible alternative and complementary approaches to the apparent incompatibility between a competition policy and the requirement to retain capability either in the national interest or (following the argument that, increasingly, national defence production runs will often become uneconomic and should be submerged in the wider collaborative search) in the interest of future European policies such as require British firms to obtain increased European links. The first is to look for the removal of obstacles to industrial co-operation in Europe so as to give a wider dimension than the national to the concept of competitiveness: the IEPG have been studying this possibility, so far without notable progress. The second is encouragement from the government to nominated major firms to move into specified areas of defence procurement in Europe, on the understanding that alternative solutions to military requirements should be sought on a competitive basis through teaming arrangements. The third is for such firms themselves, as has already happened, to assemble consortia in Europe so as to compete with other consortia for contracts from the Ministry of Defence, or even, in some cases, to seek American orders: an example of the power of such groupings is the European Small Engine Co-Operation Agreement signed in 1985 between Rolls-Royce, Turbomeca (France) and MTU (FRG), placing these firms in a commanding position for developing engines for helicopters. As the government continues to attach importance to both its competitive and its collaborative policies, there is a presumption that there is enough confidence in the viability of one or more of the above approaches to make it unnecessary to scrap one policy in favour of the other.

The political support given by Mr Heseltine and Mr Younger for the continuation of the policy of competition has been given powerful executive impetus since Mr Levene was appointed as CDP in 1984. MOD still place emphasis in SDEs on their interdependence with the defence industry in three main areas:

(a)   close association in the evolution of concepts and Staff Targets, leading to the development and procurement of equipment, competitive processes being used throughout wherever possible;

(b)   the promotion of exports of defence equipment;
(c)   the interrelationship of research activities.

Nevertheless the role of the PE has moved away, under Mr Levene's direction, from direct support of the defence industrial base and involvement with industrial policy towards what SDE 87 described as a 'hands-off' customer relationship, whereby contractors carry the full responsibility for completion of contracts and are encouraged to accept risk bearing and use private venture capital in the expectation of reward by incentives for delivering equipment on time, to specification and within cost estimates. Under this relationship, communications and monitoring become increasingly important, so that changes are fully understood by both sides. Such changes have been of great importance to the industry – for example, the end of automatic expectation of production work by design contractors and the new approach to interim payments, previously assumed, but which must now be won by achievement of agreed performance milestones. The changes were evidently so much in line with the government's overall approach to the national industry that there has been remarkably little evidence of dissatisfaction.

The list of major defence firms in Table 6.1 illustrates some essential features of the defence industry. The first is that, with the notable exception of shipbuilders (whose problems are examined in Chapter 7), the main companies identified do not depend on MOD for their survival, even though MOD may be their major customer. Also, those few of them which are currently being paid over £100 million a year by MOD include several (such as BAe, Rolls-Royce and British Shipbuilders) which have moved in this decade away from nationalised status into the private sector. Most of them are now making steady annual profits, allowing the PE to justify the move away from State support on the basis that there is no longer a financial need for such support. When Mr Levene was called to the PAC in 1987 to identify the lessons learned from the Ministry's failure to control expenditure on Nimrod,[9] he indicated an aim in future to appoint wherever possible individual prime contractors, responsible to the PE for the control of sub-contractors and for the quality and reliability of their products. These major changes in emphasis make possible a reduction of Ministry staff in certain areas, but also place the industry in a more favourable position to compete and/or collaborate successfully in Europe.

Increasingly, defence industry firms, seeing European collaboration as their best prospect for survival into the next century, are

UK-based contractors paid £5 million or more by MOD in 1985–6 [Extract from SDE 1987]

Over £250 million

British Aerospace Plc (Aircraft)
British Aerospace Plc (Dynamics)
British Shipbuilders

The General Electric Co Plc
The Plessey Co Ltd

Rolls Royce Ltd
Royal Ordnance Plc

£100–250 million

British Petroleum Co Plc
Esso UK Plc
Ferranti Plc

Hunting Associated Industries Plc
Racal Electronics Plc

Thorn-EMI Plc
Westland Plc

£50–100 million

Austin Rover Group Ltd
Dowty Group Plc
General Motors Ltd

Lucas Industries Plc
Marshall of Cambridge
    (Engineering) Ltd
Pilkington Brothers Plc

The 'Shell' Transport and
    Trading Co Plc
STC Plc

£25–50 million

BET Plc
British Airways Plc
Cossor Electronics Ltd
Digital Equipment Co Ltd
Flight Refuelling (Holdings) Plc

GKN Plc
Harland and Wolff Plc
Other British Government
    Departments
Petrofina (UK) Ltd
Philips Electronic and
    Associated Industries Ltd

Short Brothers Plc
Smiths Industries Plc
Vickers Plc

£10–25 million

BMARC Ltd
The British and Commonwealth
    Shipping Co Plc
BTR Plc
Cambridge Electronic Industries
    Plc
Conoco (UK) Ltd
Control Data Ltd
Cranfield Institute of Technology
Cray Electronics Holdings Plc
DRG Plc
Dunlop Holdings Plc

Ferguson Industrial Holdings Plc
Hawker Siddeley Group Plc
Hewlett Packard Ltd
Honeywell Ltd
Mobil Holdings Ltd
NEI Plc
Paccar UK Ltd
RCA Ltd
Remploy Ltd
The Singer Co UK Ltd

Systems Designers
    International Plc
Tate and Lyle Plc
United Scientific Holdings Plc
Vantona Viyella Plc
Volvo BM UK Ltd
The Weir Group Plc
Yarrow Plc

£5–10 million

Anglo Nordic Holdings Plc
J.C. Bamford Excavators Ltd
Bodycote International Plc
British Railways Board
British Telecommunications Plc
Cable and Wireless Plc
Cap Group Ltd
Chloride Group Plc
Courtaulds Plc
David Brown (Holdings) Ltd
Frazer Nash Group Ltd
George Blair Plc
Goodyear Tyre and Rubber Co
    (GB) Ltd

Hillsdown Holdings Plc
Humber Shiprepairers Ltd
IMB United Kingdom Holdings Ltd
Imperial Continental Gas
    Association
Inchcape Plc
John Brown Plc
Logica Ltd
Martin-Baker Aircraft Co Ltd
ML Holdings Plc
Monsanto Plc
Phicom Plc
Rank Organisation Plc
RFD Group Plc
Rockwell-Collins (UK) Ltd

Ropner Plc
Saft (United Kingdom) Ltd
Schlumberger Measurement
    and Control (UK) Ltd
Texaco Ltd
Total Oil (GB) Ltd
Trafalgar House Plc
UK Universities
Watercraft Ltd
Waverley Electronics Ltd
Wilkinson Sword Group Ltd

Notes:
1. Includes suppliers of food, fuels and services.
2. Within each financial bracket, contractors are listed in alphabetical order.
3. The status of companies in this list is that at 1 April 1985.

looking for ways of linking with Western European firms, while at the same time retaining mutually advantageous connections with the United States. Project managers for collaborative ventures, who must combine a talent for strategic control with a gift for detailed criticism, will have to be carefully selected and trained for this work, given freedom of action, simple and unbureaucratic links with higher management, and authority and standing such as the PE have found it difficult to bestow upon their own project managers. The avowed intention of the Ministry, as stated in the EFA context, is that the industry should be fitter and leaner for the future, and industry chiefs are thinking along the same lines, using a variety of processes – joint ventures, consortia and so on – to form strategic alliances with West European firms. The aims are simple and laudable: to reduce financial risk, to get better access to resources and capabilities, to improve their financial standing, to win access to new political contacts, and to use limited resources more widely in the project area. The dangers for government are as evident as the advantages to industry: there must be a risk that, as firms divide project functions between them, the resulting increased specialisation will lead to a weakening of the competitive factor. The creation of a unified European free market in 1992 will provide the occasion for inter– governmental control mechanisms to be established, especially as defence was included in EEC planning by the 1986 Single European Act, which pledges members to maintaining the technological and industrial conditions necessary for the security.

The 1990s will prove a challenging decade for the defence industry, with the wheel having turned almost full circle since the mutal suspicion between government and the industry of the 1960s. In certain areas – for example that of the maintenance of employment in politically sensitive areas, and the continuation of single sources of supply where these exist – the degree of government interest will remain high. For these areas, the policy of competition must normally take second place to political considerations. In general terms, however, it is reasonable to summarise that the decade 1977 to 1987 has seen a significant movement of responsibility for the success of defence projects away from Whitehall into the defence industry. The fact that Britain displaced in 1987 not only France but also the USSR in arms exports throughout the world, moving into second place behind the United States, inspires confidence that British defence manufacturing capabilities have so improved as to make collaboration with Britain increasingly attractive to other major

European countries. Additionally, as British firms in which defence contracts and jobs are concentrated have product ranges diversified beyond solely the defence interest (as the list of major UK-based defence contractors in Table 6.1 illustrates), it is unlikely that defence funds alone will be the criterion for maintaining their profitability. The old arguments on the need for the government to sustain a defence capability with subsidies from public funds become less relevant when the defence industry shows itself capable of standing on its own feet to this extent; nevertheless, defence work will continue to call for risk taking with advanced technology, and there will often be a case for the government to share those risks by providing financial support, provided that the industry is prepared to make a fair return for government investment in terms of sharing a percentage of profits.

Some British firms (British Aerospace, Plessey, Rolls-Royce, Ferranti and Westland are examples) have established successful European reputations as prime contractors for collaborative projects or as leading members of consortia. For others, the dilemma may remain that identified by Sir Michael Cary in the 1975 lecture quoted in the second paragraph of this chapter that 'if you happen to be "A", the firm selected for the important task of developing on behalf of the whole NATO Alliance a particular piece of equipment, you are as pleased as Punch. On the other hand, if you happen to be "B" and are told that you will be dropped out of the R&D game altogether, you are naturally displeased'.

7 The Royal Navy and Collaboration

In pre-Second World War years, and in the period up to the Thorneycroft-Healey-Mountbatten reforms of the British defence organisation in 1963/4, the Admiralty was known as 'the rogue elephant of Whitehall' – an expression used not so much with admiration and affection as in exasperation and despair! It is thus not surprising to find that procurement processes and collaborative histories for the Royal Navy are different enough from those in the other services to justify a separate chapter. The case for these differences is that the ship and its machinery, weapons and equipment are all one large package; if the ship is small and unsophisticated enough, the procurement is regarded as a one-package transaction, with all equipment and machinery procured with the hull. For larger and more sophisticated vessels, some armament and equipment will be separately developed, but their integration with the main design and development will form a required section of the staff target and staff requirement. Naval authorities pioneered the cardinal points specification (CPS) procedure outlined in the first chapter: after cardinal points have been identified, competitive tenders are invited for development and production, and assessed under criteria agreed between naval Operational Requirements Staff and the Procurement Executive. Once the staff requirement has been endorsed, procurement continues, normally using fixed price incentive contracts. The first Admiralty oiler replacement was procured from Harland and Wolff as a unit under CPS procedures, and the second is to be constructed by Swan Hunter.

With warships as the main armoury of the Royal Navy, it is not surprising that an extra co-ordinating machinery should be added to the procedures for staff targets and requirements, in that a high-level Fleet Effectiveness Committee must be satisfied before projects pass to the EPC or its sub-committee: its task, as identified to the PAC in 1986,[1] is to identify long-term warship, weapons and equipment requirements, a remit of extreme importance to the naval shipbuilding industry, which has special features which distinguish it from defence industries manufacturing aeroplanes, missiles or vehicles. Among these, one important feature is the industry's reliance on defence orders, compared with the diversification which the other major firms identified in Table 6.1 have cultivated to reduce their dependence on the MOD: the industry cannot easily market warships as private ventures, and must wait for ships to be in service with the Royal Navy before their export potential attracts overseas customers. A major problem has been the prolongation of this waiting time for the industry by a series of delays in taking decisions on future orders, for either political or budgetary reasons, delays which (according to a report in *The Independent* at the time of the 1987 Conservative Conference)[2] resulted in political fears that the future both of the warship yards and of the Royal Navy itself were being jeopardised – fears which were strengthened at the time by forecasts that the eight yards might be reduced to two by 1997: one for surface ships and one for submarines. The location of the main yards in areas of high unemployment – Belfast,[3] Clydeside, Tyneside and Mersey-side – and of extreme dependence on the local industry, (as in Barrow-in-Furness) adds election fuel to these fears. The question-mark placed over the future of the Royal Navy by the five major defence reviews of the last thirty years has not eased these fears, and there have been numerous examples in the 1980s of hesitation and budgetary delays.

The most recent examples led the PAC to begin in 1987[4] an inquiry into the future size and role of the Royal Navy's surface fleet; during early sessions the MOD admitted that reductions in the fleet had led to reductions in training and in exercise-participation, but claimed that vessels would be brought out of refit in wartime. Even before this evidence was given, the government's plans to order three new frigates a year had been abandoned, on the grounds that revised maintenance cycles made this programme no longer necessary. Yet the Defence Committee had pointed out in 1985 the importance of maintaining these order plans if the average age of destroyers and frigates were not to rise sharply,[5] and that, assuming 25 years' life per warship, 18 vessels would have to be phased out by 1991.

This uncertainty in naval planning has had its impact for naval shipbuilding at a time when the major yards were already facing profound difficulty in obtaining orders. British Shipbuilders won no significant warship orders from abroad in the decade 1977–87, and the government's decision to withdraw state support and subsidies from the warship-building yards by privatising has issued a huge challenge to the yards involved to reduce their overheads so as to survive and succeed in the private sector. The problems are evidently not confined to British yards – the IEPG report *Towards a Stronger Europe*[6] indicates that over-capacity in the shipbuilding industry, due to the virtual collapse of the civil market and the dearth of naval orders, is now so bad that it is possible that shipbuilding and fitting firms may disappear, or become very limited, as a production industry in some nations, this being a greater threat for the future than the possible penetration of the sector by the United States.

This background of government uncertainty and of orders inadequate to retain existing capacity is relevant to the history of naval collaboration in NATO. After superficial and fruitless discussions between the United States and Western European governments in the mid-1960s on the possibility of mix-manning warships in the Alliance interest, NATO settled down to the more practical idea of multinational task forces, which has worked well with the Standing Naval Force Atlantic and that for the Channel: progress was made with the standardisation of equipment and communications and with collaboration in the development of naval missile systems, but no common operational needs, linked with the coincidence of national plans and budgets, appear to have been identified in NATO until the early 1970s, when two major collaborative ventures for warships were launched. Towards the end of the 1960s, the Royal Netherlands Navy had begun studies of a future frigate, leading to the preliminary design of the Kortenaer class in 1969/70. At this point the possibility of collaboration with Britain arose, but disappeared in 1970 when the Dutch preferred their weaponry to the British Sea Wolf and wanted hull dimensions to correspond with the size of their national dry docks. So the Royal Navy moved towards the Type 22 frigate, but in 1974 a West German operational requirement broadly in line with Dutch plans was developed, and the two MODs agreed in 1975 to procure frigates on the Dutch design with common operational characteristics and some standardised equipment. The first Dutch frigate had already been ordered, and the West Germans changed much of the equipment in favour of their national products: nevertheless the venture qualified for the description of the 'NATO frigate for the 1970s' using the NATO Sea Sparrow missile system and having spare parts pooled.

At almost the same time that the two MODs reached this 1975 agreement, the French, Belgian and Netherlands MODs (after contacts between naval authorities the year before had resulted in a joint staff requirement) agreed to develop a tripartite minehunter, with features which make it a very interesting example of collaborative achievement. France would (naturally, in their view!) undertake the overall design and development of the prototype vessel and be responsible for the minehunting gear and some electronics; Belgium would cover all electrical installation; and the Netherlands would design and develop propulsion systems. The programme office was established in France, with a Frenchman directing the project as a totality. The three governments shared R&D costs, and the three national industries benefited equally from the work involved. Although no tripartite maintenance organisation was established, manuals were joint, fault analysis and modification management were unified and some spares, repair and software work was centrally organised. The French prototype was laid down in 1977 at Lorient, and commissioned in 1981 as the first of 15 ships. The Dutch started slightly later, as they built a specially-constructed 'ship factory' for the whole class, but have made such good progress with their 15 ships that they allowed the fourteenth and fifteenth to be exported to Indonesia, delaying their own ships. The Belgians, committed to buying ten with an option on five more, followed the Dutch example of a 'ship factory': as this was not constructed until 1983, their programme is behind that of the other two.

A section of Volume II of *Towards a Stronger Europe*[7] examines this minehunter as a representative naval collaborative project (the choice was not difficult!) and reproduces comments from 'a senior official closely associated with the project over a number of years'. In his general remarks, this French official claims, with good reason, that the objectives of the programme were met and that the project is successful. He accepts that, although the R&D efforts led to a superb technical solution, they were higher than would have been nationally acceptable, but balances this with the unique advantages gained by the three navies in exchanging know-how and copying each other's instructions and work methods in a variety of areas. Going on to generalise from this particular point, he makes some valid points on collaboration in general which are very relevant to the final venture to be examined in this chapter, the NFR90. His view is that:

(a)   there should be a strong and constant political interest in the project to overcome national tendencies to slip back to national rules and procedures;

(b) clusters of well-chosen participants, who complement each other, should be chosen;

(c) decision-takers should number as few as possible and three is a very efficient number;

(d) there must be a consensus on how to balance equally the economic inputs of the participants;

(e) it must be remembered that each country and even each shipyard have their own standards, specifications and methods of construction unless extra costs are to be incurred in arranging adaptation of plans at a late stage;

(f) the time taken to reach international decisions should not be underestimated – for the minehunter, they were, and this led to serious delays in construction and in the delivery of equipment.

It is of great interest that these conclusions should be drawn from a relatively unsophisticated venture with the ideal number of countries involved: the 'NATO frigate for the 1970s' cannot realistically be considered as being of the same collaborative interest – particularly in relation to NFR90 – as the minehunter, although its comparative success, taken with the greater success of the smaller vessels, may well have formed the background to the attitudes of naval authorities within NATO which led to the genesis of NFR90 in 1979. Uniquely in the history of NATO, several nations found that their frigates would need replacement in the 1990s, even though their initial positions on what was needed and how it would be used were widely different. The initial assumption was made – doubtless based on the precedents of the 1970s – that each nation would build its own warships, and use the equipment of its choice: the hope was for common savings at the production stage and reduced costs once ships were commissioned, as a result of logistics savings. After an outline staff target had been formulated, industrial interests were (very sensibly) brought in through the NIAG machinery, and an industrial subgroup was established in 1981 to prepare a pre-feasibility study. At this time the participating nations were Belgium, Canada, France, the Federal Republic, Italy, the Netherlands, Norway, the United Kingdom and the United States.

The subgroup made its report in October 1982, using the input of over 150 engineers from over 50 companies and recommending that a technical and economic solution was feasible, but pointing out that cost savings would be available only if all ships ordered were identical: the purchase initially assumed was for about 150 ships excluding exports, (although this has now been reduced) and the first ship was to be commissioned in 1992 to meet the requirements of the West German Navy. The following April, after Belgium and Norway had decided to withdraw but Spain had acceded, the eight participating nations agreed to proceed to an equally-funded feasibility study, whose main objectives were to examine possible designs, compare estimates with likely costs if participators 'went it alone', identify work shares and evaluate areas of risk. For the purpose, an International Joint Venture Company (IJVC) was established, consisting of the nominated firms from each country which would take the lead for that country. At about the same time, a Project Management Office was set up, with two representatives of each country: legal and contractual expertise was to be provided by West Germany, as host nation for the project, an arrangement which might appear questionable to the PAC in terms of financial accountability but provides an alternative solution to establishing a large number of internationally-paid lawyers and contract staff in an international headquarters.

Feasibility study ended in November 1985, and the preparation of an agreed NATO staff requirement began, in discussion with the NATO major military commanders; additionally, a programme of national work during project definition was prepared, it being recognised that participators would see this as the critical stage for decisions to proceed. A Statement of Intent to proceed with the project was signed in July 1986, but Britain entered caveats (believed to relate to the need for a common approach to the installation of an air defence weapons system, which had not emerged between November and July), and this led to a long delay before Britain agreed to sign the MOU which would enable project development to proceed. Six of the participators had agreed to sign this MOU before the CNAD met in October 1987, to complete the formalities, but Britain and France reserved their position, although accepting a concept exploration phase for the development of an air defence weapons system. SDE87 had reflected government doubts, indicating that NFR90 'could eventually replace our Type 42 destroyers'. From October onwards, there were well-authenticated Press reports of a battle between MOD and the Treasury over whether Britain should sign the MOU before a weapons system had been identified. After Cabinet Committee discussion, Mr Younger reported to the House of Commons in January 1988 that, despite concern over the co-ordination of the work on the frigate with that on the principal armament system, Britain had agreed to sign the MOU, but with an option for later withdrawal; France had followed the British example.

The continuation of both the ship and the weapons systems projects is of obvious value to the defence industry: nine leading British contractors have formed a registered group (Supermarine Consortium Limited) as the British section of the IJVC, and will apply powerful pressure on the government for continuation beyond project definition. If Treasury pressure is again mounted at the end of project definition, these nine firms might find it necessary to put their own money into the early part of the development stage, to enable the project's momentum to be maintained. In any case, the results of the delays which have been experienced in the 1980s are that the prototype vessel is very unlikely to be commissioned in 1992, as originally planned – the slippage in the programme may well be as much as four years – and that the risk that participators will *not* order identical vessels has increase.

Applying this history to the comments made by the French and recorded above, it seems clear that to move so far away from the 'efficient' number of three decision-takers as eight or nine participators is to increase enormously the risk of delays in the decision-taking process and consequently in the planned in-service dates. Also essential actions such as the co-ordination of the hulls with the weapons system seem to have been deferred so as to call for a minimum need for political agreement. On the other hand, expensive management structures have been avoided and, so far, there seems a good chance that the economic and industrial benefits will be shared out fairly between the participators, as happened with the mine-hunter: this would be jeopardised, however, if each nation finally decided to construct a national variant, as the cost savings were hypothesised on the assumption of identical ships. A main lesson (remembering the British delays in 1987) is that political will has to be manifested, for a collaborative project which is believed to make economic sense, earlier than at the project definition stage, through clear involvement with such essential initial assumptions as operational plans, design options and the technical risk which is acceptable.

8 Case-Studies in Collaboration

Before taking a final look, in the next chapter, at the collaborative arena in general terms, I have selected two brief case-studies out of the many examples available to illustrate some of the particular difficulties experienced over the last thirty years in areas which at first glance seem ideal for collaboration. The first links the postwar history of the Royal Ordnance Factories (ROF) with the fate of attempts to develop bilaterally a main battle tank (MBT) for deployment in Western Europe. The second studies the mixed fortunes experienced by government and industry in developing collaborative helicopters.

I. THE ROYAL ORDNANCE FACTORIES AND THE MAIN BATTLE TANK

To a layman like myself, collaboration in MBT development would seem not too difficult: as with a car and an aeroplane, a tank is an assembly task, for which distribution of work shares should not prove too complicated. In military terms, with the Western European task identical and the advantages for Allied armies of standardisation being self-evident, a strong impetus toward collaboration might be expected from NATO military leaders. For leaders of NATO governments, collaboration between a minimum of two member countries leading to joint development and/or production could be held up as a dramatic justification of Alliance policies. Finally, for the United Kingdom, the existence up to the end of 1984 within the Ministry of Defence of an organisation (the Royal Ordnance Factories) capable of developing and producing tanks to execute a political and military requirement provided the means for the British government to control the execution of a collaborative policy – for example with France, where the construction facility was also under State control, although, after France's self-removal from NATO's military integrated structure, the prospect of French collaboration in developing an MBT with another Alliance country was admittedly bleak.

The value of the ROF's contribution to the national effort in the Second World War is adequately assessed in Official War Histories.[1] In 1939, the 'historic' factories (Woolwich, dating from the seventeenth century, which had become Britain's largest factory in the inter-war years, Waltham Abbey, tracing its origins back to Elizabethan days as the Royal Gunpowder Factory; and Enfield, which began producing muskets in 1811) had been supplemented by six new factories, which the government had approved, to their credit, in the mid-1930s; two more (Bishopston and Bridgwater) had also been approved, but did not start production until 1940 and 1941 respectively. By the end of 1939, approval had been given to a further 14 factories: by the end of 1940 25 were operating, with about 110 000 in the total ROF workforce, and in mid-1942, at the peak of British munitions production, there were 44 factories, employing over 300 000. The factories were functionally divided into three broad groupings: fillings, explosives and propellants, and engineering; the last-named group included the wide range of production tasks connected with metal engineering, from ammunition through small arms to guns and their mountings. In 1943, it occurred to an unidentified minister that the ROFs ought to be producing tanks: accordingly, the factory at Leeds (which had been turning out guns since 1939) was converted in 1944 into a tank factory for the manufacture of Centurions. Up to that time, in the judgement of the Official Historian, 'in most warlike stores except tanks, the role assigned to the ROFs was that of first starter' – in other words, the government looked first to the ROFs for the production of the munitions falling within their capacity. To quote again, the ROFs 'were conceived as very great undertakings indeed' and 'their participation in all major armaments manufacture brought very substantial advantages'.

In 1942, a Select Committee on National Expenditure recommended that the ROFs should be contained in a single organisation comprising all functions necessary to their operation, and regarded as a self-contained group. To an extent, this corporate approach had been that of King George V, who had bestowed the title 'Royal' in 1930 when the three 'historic' factories formed the basis of the organisation. Inevitably, by 1945, capacity was far exceeding demand, and at least half of the ROFs were declared redundant almost immediately after the end of the war. The organisation, under War Office control until 1939, had then fallen under the wing of the Ministry of Supply. When that Ministry was disbanded in 1959, the

War Office regained control and retained it until the Procurement Executive was established in 1971. As a part of the new, commercially-orientated approach of the Rayner reforms, the ROFs became, in 1973, the first government organisation to operate under a trading fund: the broad implication was that the Treasury accepted that the engineers and accountants within the organisation should produce consolidated profit and loss accounts, with the Treasury taking an annual dividend. Through all these postwar reorganisations, the number of factories had dwindled until, when the Conservative administration won power in 1979, there were eleven factories, divided between the dual functions of weapons and fighting vehicles (including the Leeds factory), and ammunition, with a total workforce of about 20 000. The new government decided quickly on privatisation of the ROFs, and a chairman was appointed from International Business Machines (IBM) to prepare the organisation for the private sector. The propellants and explosives establishments at Westcott and Waltham Abbey were transferred to the ROFs as a basis for R&D effort. After enabling legislation had been passed in 1984, and an escape route operated for those wishing to stay in the Ministry of Defence, the ROFs were incorporated under the Companies Act as Royal Ordnance plc in January 1985. Consistently with the 1942 Select Committee recommendation, the government aimed to float the organisation as a group.

At this point of a necessarily brief historical sketch, I return to the fortunes of Leeds as a tank factory, and to the attempts made before 1979 to initiate MBT collaboration. Starting with the latter, all initiatives had proved abortive, beginning in the late 1950s with France and the FRG, proceeding through the 1960s and the 1970s with attempts between the United States and the FRG, and between the United Kingdom and the FRG, to agree upon MBT '70: time-scales and requirements between the interested nations could not be matched, and – it would seem almost in despair – the Labour administration of the late 1970s decided that MBT '80 should be all-British. The consequent story will be familiar to tank enthusiasts, but must be summarised for the sake of completion.

Having, up to the time of the trading fund in 1973, always had to share UK tank orders with others, notably Vickers,[2] the ROFs decided to design a Chieftain variant (the 900) at Leeds as a private venture for the export market alone; this was presumably regarded by the Treasury as an enterprising use of public funds, but the venture was to be ill-starred. By 1982, two prototypes had been completed, but in 1985 the 900 was quietly removed from offer. This compounded the almost disastrous history of orders from Iran for an improvement on Chieftain to follow the total of about 900 Chieftains delivered: when the (initially lucrative) contract came to a sudden end in 1979, the varients known as Shir I and II had no apparent British use, but the Treasury dividend was rescued by a large Jordanian order, which was met in the form of the Khalid tank, using Shir material. Subsequently, with MBT '80 in mind, Shir II was used for the preparation of the Challenger, which went into project definition in 1978: with privatisation in mind, the Ministry of Defence announced that Challenger would be ordered from Leeds for the British Army, an announcement which brought prestige not only to Leeds but to the other ten ROFs, all of which had an interest in providing components, armaments, ammunition and propellants for Challenger; the engines are manufactured by Rolls-Royce. The first off production was handed over to the Army in 1983 and, in the same year, Leeds (as well as Alvis and Vickers) was given a study contract for MBT '95. As this time the MBT to be developed stood a far better chance of being collaborative with FRG than in the previous attempts, the company-to-be seemed to have an excellent opportunity not only of being a prime contractor again for a Ministry of Defence order, but of being a prime contractor in a collaborative tank venture, a prize which had hitherto escaped an organisation which had, however, been frequently involved in a lesser role in collaborative work on guns and missiles. (The new company's then Director of Operations admitted, in an interview with *Jane's Defence Weekly* in October 1986, that the organisation had not been successful at collaboration.)

However, nemesis had withdrawn from the scene only temporarily. Mr Peter Levene had given wide publicity in 1985 to his emphasis on competition in defence orders, and the chairman of Vickers Defence Systems, the main rival of Leeds, argued successfully that to give the defence market no chance of competing for individual ROFs was an abnegation of the government's policy. Bowing to this logic, the government sold off Leeds to Vickers in 1986 at an extremely reasonable price. Deprived of the jewel in their crown, Royal Ordnance plc had no longer any chance of being successfully floated and, after an appropriate competition which turned finally into a two-horse race between British Aerospace and GKN, was taken over by British Aerospace in 1987; the outcome is probably in the national interest, in that both Vickers and British Aerospace have excellent export and collaborative records compared with those of Royal Ordnance plc.

The outcome of the Army's Project Foresight in 1987 was to conclude that, on balance, the tank is still viable as a battlefield weapon. The British Army must replace its 500 Chieftains and the FRG Army its Leopard IIs by the turn of the century; the available options are off-the-shelf purchase of the FRG Leopard or US Abrams M-IAI, or more (and improved) Challengers. Against the background of the study contracts issued in 1983, a decision will probably be taken in 1988.[3] For the next century, a new collaborative MBT is a possibility. The outcome of land and air collaboration with the FRG to date has been encouraging, and a decision on tank collaboration (which would involve a compromise between the two countries on the tank gun and the time-scales, and a judgement when a new-technology gun might be available) would link Britain firmly once more in a major project with a partner of great industrial strength. Vickers at once partnered with Krauss-Mattei in 1983 for the study contract, and they would be well placed to plan an MBT on a collaborative basis which would bear comparison with off-the-shelf purchases or a Mark II Challenger: perhaps, at last, the tank factory at Leeds will find a major collaborative role!

An interesting aspect of this brief case-study is the admitted failure of this large engineering organisation to achieve success in collaborative ventures even though its activities were controlled by successive Ministers and Secretaries of State for Defence in the period up to its departure from the public sector at the end of 1984. The reader must choose between possible explanations:

(a) that the higher direction of the Ministry did not believe the organisation capable of taking a leading role in collaboration;

(b) that successive governments did not think it appropriate for a government unit to take such a role;

(c) that the Army operational requirements staffs, during the years when collaboration was succeeding in the aircraft and missiles areas, did not find particular projects for the future which could be undertaken by the organisation;

(d) that the higher direction of the Army during these years preferred national development and manufacture to the potential risks of collaboration effort.

II. THE HELICOPTER AS A COLLABORATIVE PROJECT

The helicopter is an obviously suitable vehicle for European collaboration, because its value throughout the world in a wide variety of military and civil roles means that there is a market for a wide variety of types, and because its manufacture can be divided with relative ease between partners producing airframes, engines, sonar, radar, processing and display systems, tail pylons, stabiliser modules and so on and weapons; equally, the assembly of the aircraft's parts can be done by one partner after manufacture by another. Admittedly, for larger and more sophisticated vehicles, initial capital costs to launch a new model are high – and private ventures in consequence risky, as Westland plc found with the Westland 30, which was not a commercial success.

Gardner and Longstaff have described the slow development of interest in Britain in military helicopters in the years after the Second World War, when production was an American-dominated activity.[4] In the early 1950s, as helicopters became more reliable, their value to defence and to the economy was increasingly evident, and independent production began in Britain, using the experience gained through production under licence of American designs. Westland quickly became the largest manufacturer in Europe, but collaboration within Western Europe was not found feasible until, in 1962, the French Army decided upon a requirement for a dual-role helicopter (medium-sized tactical assault/logistics transport), which was designed as the SA330, the first model flying in April 1965. As indicated in Chapter 2, the mid-1960s were a crucial period for the first real British interest in military collaboration, and the successful flight of the SA330 was well-timed from this point of view. Also the French had made progress with the development of the SA340, a lighter, five-seater helicopter for Army observation/reconnaissance, and Sud Aviation (later to be Aérospatiale) were working with a Westland design team by 1963 towards developing a collaborative aircraft. Joint staff talks, and discussion on the Anglo-French Steering Committee, identified an RAF and Royal Marine (RM) requirement in line with the SA330, and an Army requirement in line with SA340 plans, and what became the Anglo-French helicopter package had begun to take shape.

In Britain, Westland began in 1963 the development of the WG3 (later called WG13) as one of three new helicopters, of which it proved the only success. Its potential as a utility/anti-submarine warfare (ASW)/reconnaissance/anti-tank helicopter was attractive to the French. In May 1965, the two governments agreed to collaborate in the development and production of military helicopters, and detailed talks between experts led to ministerial agreement, in February 1967, that the French should have the main responsibility for assembling the components of the SA330 (Puma), with Westland making certain parts, and Rolls-Royce contributing parts of the engines for the 48 aircraft ordered by Britain, as for the other helicopters in the package. France would continue to develop the SA340 (designated Gazelle, as the SA341, at the pre-production stage); the French-built prototype flew in 1967, and the Westland prototype in 1970. Britain produced components for the French prototype, and the first production models flew in France in 1971, and in Britain in 1972. For the WG13 (Lynx), Britain retained design leadership: the 1967 agreement was more complicated for the Lynx than for the other aircraft, with five variants specified – two for the French Army and Navy, three for the Royal Navy, RAF and British Army. Production was to be shared 70 per cent by Westland and 30 per cent by Aérospatiale; a final governmental agreement in April 1968, confirmed production arrangements for the three aircraft, and Puma assembly began at Westland in 1969.

The defence correspondent of *The Economist* regards this early collaborative agreement as one of the best of the collaborative approaches tried since 1957,[5] and his judgement is borne out, in military terms, by the comments of specialist writers: more than 2500 aircraft were produced in the 20 years between 1968 and 1987. Mr Everett-Heath[6] praises the Gazelle's manoeuvrability, speed and endurance, as demonstrated in the Falklands campaign, but refers to its vulnerability: he assesses it as 'a tremendous success as a joint Anglo/French project between the 1970s and 1980s'. It is still in service with the Army Air Corps and, for aircraft training, with the Royal Navy. Successive SDEs have illustrated the all-round value of RAF Pumas (for example, after the Mexico City earthquake in 1985 and the Jamaican floods in 1986) and, with their long-standing NATO role for tactical air-lift logistic support soon to pass to a variant of the EH101 (of which more later), they will take over the transport role of the Wessex, which began production almost thirty years ago and in itself indicates the long life expected of service helicopters. Puma also has had an impressive sales success, especially in ex-French colonies.

The Lynx deserves a paragraph to itself as the most versatile of the three helicopters – and the one which led to considerable friction between the partners. It had been agreed between the two governments in 1967 that the French Navy would take the aircraft for ASW and liaison roles, and the French Army for reconnaissance and anti-tank roles. In 1969, after the Lynx had been experiencing severe development problems, the French anti-tank requirement was cancelled, although the French Navy placed an order in 1974 for the ASW version, using French sonar. It is noteworthy that the sales of the naval version have been more successful than those of the land variant: it is useful to have French expertise and ruthlessness on one's side in the export of military systems![7] This ruthlessness was exemplified when, France having backed out of the commitment to the land varient, Westland's partners, Aérospatiale, began developing the Dauphin, whose military variant Panther is a rival to the Lynx in the land assault/transport/anti-tank role. Returning, though, to the Lynx, it has found favour with the Army, the Royal Navy and the Royal Marines: although some early models were intended for the RAF, they were cancelled before 1972. Gardner and Longstaff consider that the Lynx 'was unique in incorporating several new features, which greatly enhanced its operational capabilities as a self-contained weapon system', and Everett-Heath estimates that the naval version will remain in service until at least 1997, and the Army version until five years later: the Lynx experience was the basis for Westland's private venture development of the Lynx 3 and Westland 30.

An interesting final comment on the helicopter package comes from *The Economist*'s defence correspondent's article already quoted: he points out that neither development nor components production was duplicated for any of the three aircraft, and that no 'supranational bureaucracy' (such as has been found useful/necessary in other collaborative ventures) was involved; he estimated that, for the Tornado, the extra layers of administration involved hundreds of people whose salaries, offices, travel, meeting costs and other expenses added significantly to the cost of the aircraft. On the debit side of the helicopter package, however, is the Westland experience with the Lynx of French attitudes at that time – both in cancellations and in the parallel development of Dauphin. Professor Freedman has adjudged that this experience became an impediment to attempts at collaboration between Westland and Aérospatiale in subsequent years.[8]

In West Germany, Bolköw had begun in 1962 (the year in which they merged with Messerschmitt) the development of the helicopter which was to become the successful BO105, used by the FRG Army for liaison/observation/anti-tank roles. Between the dates of its flight in 1967 and first production in 1972, a further merger had led to the inauguration of the powerful company MBB. In Italy, Agusta (working after the Second World War in close collaboration with the Americans) was by the 1970s designing its own helicopters. The multiple efforts of the four countries in developing different aircraft for the same roles cried out for a collaborative approach, and an early success of the IEPG was to sow the seed for the joint declaration in 1978 by the four governments in favour of European helicopter collaboration. Ten years after that declaration, however, the results must be assessed as disappointing. Progress made to the end of 1987 is summarised below.

France/FRG

The concept of a common anti-tank helicopter (CATH) – also known as PAH2 – was initiated in the mid-1970s, but formal planning was delayed until 1984. Thereafter, incompatibility of requirements followed by FRG budget difficulties delayed the programme, although it was given renewed political support in November 1987. French and FRG companies, with Rolls-Royce, will provide the engines for an estimated 400 aircraft and, provided that the political support is not withdrawn, the project will probably survive.

France/Italy/Spain/Netherlands

Feasibility studies for the NH90 ASW and tactical transport helicopter ended in October 1986. At that time, Britain was a partner, but withdrew in April 1987: the Army decided that the 15-man transportability of the NH90 was inadequate. Italy is responsible for the ASW models and France for the transport version. The market is seen as about 700 helicopters, with production beginning in 1993, but, with four-nation involvement presenting greater management problems than in the Anglo-French deal, this date may well slip. The Westland-produced Black Hawk could still be a serious competitor for West European orders, and this can be seen as placing Britain in an invidious position *vis-à-vis* the four other European countries developing the NH90.

Britain/Italy/Spain/Netherlands

By the early 1980s, the governments of the four countries (initially Britain and Italy) were discussing ideas for a light attack helicopter, called Tonal after the Aztec god of war. It was agreed in 1987 to plan for 225 helicopters to be in service by the mid-1990s, developed by the Joint European Helicopter Company. It was found by the four countries that their requirements differed too widely from CATH to make amalgamation possible. Tonal will be based on the Agusta A129 anti-tank variant: if it runs into difficulties the prospects of CATH in Europe will improve and the Americans will be quick to put forward their LHX helicopter as another alternative for Western Europe. A major problem, as with the NH90, will be to ensure continuing support from all four partners – already in 1988, a Parliamentary defence committee in the Netherlands was insisting that the US Apache should be evaluated before the Netherlands Parliament considers orders for Tonal.

Britain/Italy

In 1979, Agusta and Westland announced the formation of a joint company, European Helicopter Industries (EHI), to design, develop and manufacture a new helicopter (EH101) for which the two governments signed an MOU that November. An initial difficulty was that EHI was not allowed authority as a prime contractor, and this must have increased problems of planning and control. The EH101 has been ordered by the Royal Navy (to replace Sea King) and by the Army in its troop-carrying role. The helicopter may be in service by 1993; in addition to its ASW and troop-carrying roles, it has value as a surveillance and Air Search and Rescue (ASR) aircraft, as well as for commercial use. A main problem for this £500 million development programme (which began with joint naval studies in the early 1970s leading up to a ministerial agreement for collaboration in 1978) may well be the continuing capability of Westland – a relatively small firm – to match the management demands of the development and/or production of helicopters in three separate groups: EH101, Tonal and Black Hawk. Already in 1986, at the time of the political crisis surrounding the future of Westland, there were alleged to be indications that Agusta might look for another partner. Now that over one hundred EH101s have been ordered initially by the two governments, and that the helicopter has been selected by Canada (up to 50 aircraft) as its new shipborne aircraft, the 1986 difficulty has been lessened, but the division of interest remains between the European-based projects and the Black Hawk, which is the obvious competitor for the European NH90.

Currently there are some 3500 Western European military heli-copters and 10 000 American; the industry in Western Europe produced 1100 helicopters in the years 1974–84. Military aircraft deliveries have been forecast as between 600 and 700 a year over the next decade.[9] A renewed effort to reduce existing duplications was made in 1987, when the 1978 joint declaration was revived and widened in the formation of a European Helicopter Collaboration (EHC) with members from Britain, France, Germany, Italy and, subsequently, the Netherlands and Spain. This mini-group within the IEPG will exchange information on staff requirements at expert level, leading up to an EHC meeting in the autumn of 1988 to examine possibilities to be put forward for the harmonisation of requirements, time-scales and industrial planning. So, although for-tunes for governments and industries have indeed been mixed over the 25 years of helicopter collaboration, the aircraft remains probably the most hopeful area for integrated European progress in the military field – even should this movement imply that, in the long term, Westland, the only British manufacturer, might become a subsidiary of a continental firm: with the dismantling of physical, fiscal and technical barriers between EEC members in 1992, and the opening of the Channel Tunnel in 1993, this may seem less alarming a prospect in five years than it is for some at the present time.

Whatever the future, the verdict on the decade since the 1978 declaration of intent must be that opportunities were missed by the Western European countries manufacturing helicopters. The two main reasons have been a failure to harmonise operational require-ments and a lack of political will at ministerial level to insist on such harmonisation, if only in the interest of the worldwide market for helicopters – even small third-world countries accept the helicopter in a variety of (relatively new) roles, both military and civilian: the

anti-terrorist capacity and the value in agriculture and in search/
rescue operations are obvious examples. The United States has
evident advantages in its huge manufacturing capacity and in that,
like the USSR, its military requirements are met without the need to
associate with collaborative partners. The United Kingdom can at
least claim to have played a major role in seeking to achieve
harmonisation in the common interest; Mr Heseltine made a valiant
but unsuccessful attempt in 1985 to bring together the separate
planning for the Tonal and CATH aircraft; on the other hand,
Britain's rejection in 1986 of the European consortium proposal for
Westland's future in favour of the American option, and the subsequent withdrawal from the NH90 group, were seen by potential
European partners as a move away from the 1985 position. The EHC
group survives, however, and its Autumn 1988 meeting may yet
provide an opportunity for the Euro-optimism which seemed to have
been born with the Anglo/French co-operation of the 1960s.

For Westland plc, it is critically important that the EH101 succeeds
in achieving the global sales forecast by the company in evidence to
the Defence Committee in 1986, that is, over 1000 vehicles over the
next 25 years: helicopter sales form about 65 per cent of the
company's total sales, and Black Hawk has not yet proved successful
in commercial terms. Apart from the financial aspects for the
company, its future standing for European collaborative projects to
cover the development of vehicles for the next century will probably
depend also on the success of the EH101, especially if Tonal fails to
compete with the Franco–German and American alternatives. It is
within the bounds of possibility that, in the next century, European
military helicopter production will be shared between the French and
Germans on the one hand, and the British and Italians on the other.

9 Problems, Partners and People

PROBLEMS

Collaboration presents formidable problems in many areas, even when the early difficulties of finding commonality of views (on objectives, time-scales, technology and costs) have been overcome. Ideally, a project will be agreed before final national decisions are taken in these four areas, but this evidently becomes more difficult to achieve if more than one or two partners are in mind. These early discussions between military and civilians (from both government and industry) demand an assurance of national financial support and a readiness to compromise and show flexibility which, again, will be harder to achieve if more than two partners are involved. So partners are themselves a problem even in these initial stages, although as a factor of their number rather than of their national characteristics.

Additionally, major projects will often incorporate sizeable variants, derivatives or subsystems, which must be foreseen and planned in these early stages, and an attempt must be made to match requirements where other projects are affected: for example, the NATO Helicopter of the 1990s (NH90) project, at present in the project definition phase as a basic aircraft, may later be adopted for use with the NFR90, so planners of the helicopter will need also to keep watch on the progress of the frigate. To co-ordinate all these areas of potential difficulty, keeping always in mind not only military time-scales but the industrial availability of participating nations, (when development and production can be aligned with other national and international projects, civil as well as military) obviously demands skills and abilities of a high order for the leaders of the project, whether they are government staff or defence industry representatives. Equally, firms involved will be watching the progress of rival developments planned within approximately the same time-scale – for example, the controversial French decision to develop a national fighter in parallel and in rivalry with the collaborative EFA.

Let us assume that these early obstacles have been surmounted, and that ministerial approval has been given for participation in a collaborative project, so that we may survey the kind of problems which now lie ahead before a first memorandum of understanding (MOU) between the partners can be established, to record the major arrangements which are essential to the project's future. An MOU is not a legally-binding document, but is signed by each participating nation at an appropriately high Defence level, so that months of careful drafting by officials will be necessary to cover adequately the detailed key aspects of the project. Some European countries retain teams of skilled MOU negotiators, others (including the United Kingdom) regard the task as an administrative responsibility, but without accepting it as a career specialisation. As mentioned in Chapter 4, the NATO preference is for general MOUs which set out overall objectives and identify some specific provisions expected to apply throughout the project, but a respectable alternative is to negotiate a series of MOUs which cover the detailed arrangements for each stage of a project through its procurement cycle. Here at once, however, is a major difficulty for a collaborative programme – the time, cost and staff effort which is inevitably dedicated to these preliminary stages which, repeated at each stage of the project, add up to a longer time-scale for development and production compared with national projects. So there is a fine balance for consideration by military authorities between the foreseen longer time-scale of the project, with the risk that technology involved will be obsolete by the time that production is reached, and the greater security for its future which is built in as a result of international reluctance to abandon projects which have involved such careful diplomatic preparation.

The major items forming part of an MOU package (apart from objectives which are specific to particular projects) are of such importance as to merit examination under separate subheadings, in the order of their importance and nuisance value. The responsibility for the co-ordination of the parts falls, within MOD, to the project manager, who will often delegate it to the financial representatives in his team; for defence industry, the prime contractor (under arrangements described in Chapter 6) will carry the responsibility for co-ordination.

Management Structures

Over the history of the last twenty years of collaborative projects, a variety of management structures has been tried out, and their advantages and disadvantages have become well-known, to the extent that, depending on the nature of the project and its size and complexity, particular structures should easily be found to match particular projects. Unfortunately this is where national susceptibilities are quickly aroused! The choice is broadly between an international agency, with responsibility for a total system to a policy steering group of nations, or an organisation of participating nations themselves, in which either one leader is identified or the responsibility for subsystems divided among participators, with one nation co-ordinating; if this latter option is adopted, the national defence procurement organisation will oversee the contractual commitments for the subsystems. If the 'international agency' route is followed, NATO Council authority will normally be needed to bestow upon the agency a legal authority for entering into contracts: the agency then takes the status of a NATO production and logistics organisation, and its operating expenses are shared between member nations under the same formula as their project cost contributions. Herein lies the rub, in that operating expenses for such agencies (for example, for NAMMA, the agency for Tornado and for NEFMA, the agency for the European Fighter Aircraft) can be high: national staff who are allocated to the agency receive tax-free salaries and their governments, as well as paying these salaries, must also pay the salaries of the staff who take the national posts of those who leave to join the agency.

Additionally, some nations – particularly France – are reluctant to surrender executive responsibility for a project to an agency: on the other hand, they may well be reluctant, on grounds of national prestige, to allow another nation to take the overall lead. Both Britain and France regard themselves as the natural leaders of any joint projects in which their respective interests coincide, and whichever nation finally provides the site for a project's management and contracting organisation feels that points have been won. Even if organisation is through a joint project office (eg TRIGAT), the fact that the office is in one country gives that country a tactical advantage in the distribution of key posts – which will include secretarial and interpreting/translation posts – along with the priceless asset of transacting business under the laws of that country, TRIGAT has not been an ideal organisation, it being far more difficult to divide project work in three ways between Britain, France and Germany than to hand over prime contractor responsibility to one country, as has happened with Germany for the MLRS project. Similarly with the defence industry; when, for example, British Aerospace and Marconi Defence Systems formed a joint company with the German AEG and MBB firms in July 1987 to compete for European manufacture of the AMRAAM, it was to the advantage of the British firms to have agreed that the new company's headquarters should be in England: it will often be sensible, if a company is chosen to lead in a project, for the project office to be situated in that company's nation.

Industry faces a comparable choice of options in organising contractors and subcontractors for a project. Either a conglomerate company can be formed (as with Panavia for Tornado and Eurofighter/Eurojet Turbo for the EFA), or a highly artificial network of companies, sometimes existing only on paper, can be created. Alternatively, firms can organise themselves into consortia or joint companies, preferably under the lead of one firm identified as the prime contractor. To identify such a preference indicates a different problem of the processes of collaboration: although the British procurement system has moved towards a policy of appointing prime contractors, as described in Chapter 6, not all European partners follow the same policy, and it may call for persuasion both by government and industry representatives before this and other competitive policies are agreed and acceptable. The only major failure of a collaborative project in the last decade has been the SP70, developed by Britain, the FRG and Italy on the basis of the gunnery system of the successful FH70 and accepted as a NATO project in 1973, with the FRG as project leader. More than a year before its cancellation in October 1986, CDEC had told the Public Accounts Committee that (after twelve years' experience!) he felt that the project should have been placed under the control of a German company as single prime contractor, with total responsibility for the system. So, in future, British delegates will be able to quote this precedent for the value of identifying an industrial prime contractor, involved in defining the future system from its early days. This is not to place the blame for the failure on the FRG, as the PAC criticised the MOD fiercely for inadequate preparation of plans and underestimation of costs. Equally, the traditional British readiness to compromise may not be shared by other participants, and this may be especially difficult if one or other participant seeks to change specifications or in-service dates after the project has begun.

Defence firms in Western Europe have a long record of versatility in seeking links and licensing arrangements with each other; Anthony Sampson has described the arms industry as having become, by the early years of this century 'the most international industry in the world.'[1] So, with or without prime contractors, industry should have fewer difficulties than governments in forming into competing or collaborating groups – for example, in competing for the development of a radar for the EFA, Ferranti have joined one European consortium and GEC/Marconi another, with the French and the Americans keenly interested in either competing or collaborating. The aim of the rival consortia (apart from the profit motive) is common: to establish and maintain a European radar capability strong enough to rival that of the United States.

The Management Plan

A management plan is the basic ingredient of any defence project, covering in as much detail as possible the progress to feasbility study and, in outline, the plan for development and production. If it is carefully prepared and drafted, the project stands a good chance of success: the more it is unclear or imprecise, the greater the chance that money and time will be wasted. The initial plan will require updating at later stages, essentially in the preparation of a development cost plan (DCP) and a programme for production. Such planning is difficult enough nationally, but collaboration adds extra complexities in establishing compromises between national requirements in military, financial and technological terms or, where harmonisation cannot be satisfactorily achieved, in deciding upon national variants for joint projects. Yet, unless such difficulties are surmounted at an early stage – and the discussion of concepts is ideally the point at which compromises should be reached – the partners may ultimately be faced with disagreeable negotiations, such as took place in 1986 on the SP70, with each of the participators faced with the financial and industrial consequences of cancellation. As mentioned above, the Public Accounts Committee noted that development cost plans were not prepared in sufficient detail, an that cost information was either submitted late or could not be related to the cost profile in the DCP or to the technical progress of the project. A lesson must be that participating governments and industries should monitor at a high level the progress of major projects, to ensure that milestones are regularly reviewed, costs checked and every effort made to counterbalance in this way the major disadvantage that the key staff engaged on the project are likely to be replaced during the years before production is attained.

Assuming that management structures and interfaces have been decided, the remaining items for the plan will be:

- clear objectives;
- work and cost-sharing arrangements;
- milestones for the project;
- resources which each partner is to provide;
- indications of how technological aspects are to be co-ordinated;
- agreed dates by which each partner accepts meeting their responsibilities;
- arrangements for providing management with information in the national languages accepted.

Costs, Work-Sharing, Finance, Contracts and IPR

Of the problems involved in collaboration, those concerned with finance and its implications for national governments and their employment policies are likely to prove not the least difficult for project managers, not only because of the number of financial years which will be committed to a project. How, for example, could those who drew up agreements for collaborative projects in the late 1970s have foreseen that the Ministry of Defence would be driven to impose a year's moratorium on equipment spending in 1981, with its consequential effects on development and production? Equally, a defence company may suddenly experience financial problems which impose new constraints on a project with which they are involved. A recent example was that Britain and the FRG discovered, in August 1987, unforeseen problems over payment for contractors involved with the EFA; British Aerospace, as prime contractor, planned to borrow from banks to fund development for times when government payments had not been made (that is, before milestones had been reached) but, after the German firm MBB had shown a considerable financial deficit in 1986, FRG authorities began to look for arrangements which, if MBB found it hard to obtain banking loans, would shelter the government from financial subsidies to the firm.[2] Projects may be delayed at any stage while national MODs make up their minds as to whether they can really be afforded after the latest round of budget cuts, or national MODs may suddenly dispute funding with the companies concerned just when a crucial stage is about to be reached: recent examples of both problems have been with the EFA and ASRAAM.

At the MOU stage, the most likely cause of dispute between partners is over the methodology to be used for cost and work sharing. Over the past decade, however, some broad principles have been worked out for application to the sharing of costs and work. Either the project is considered *in toto*, with costs and work shared following an agreed formula (for example, the percentage of finished equipment which each country agrees to take), or the work is divided into identifiable parts and each partner takes on the cost of their part. Alternatives are to divide the work parts under the second system by an agreed formula or, if all else fails, to accept some arbitrary approach, such as letting costs lie where they fall, at least before the development stage is reached: thus, for the EH101 and EFA, costs have been allowed to lie where they fell during development.

Cost and work-sharing arrangements form only a part of the overall funding negotiations whose results will be shown in the MOU. Partners must decide if each is to fund only the work done by its own industry or take on a percentage of the funding of the whole project. Additionally, the MOU must record the whole range of arrangements to be made for payment and their authorisation – which for a NATO project will be audited not only by national authorities but also by the NATO Board of Auditors – and show plans for changes in exchange or inflation rates and for the treatment of taxes, duties, insurance liabilities and indemnities.

The strategy for contracts to appear in the MOU will normally be chosen between the alternatives of national placements within national industries or, if the system of a prime contractor is followed, by one of the partners with that contractor – or with an international consortium. Each method has its obvious advantages and disadvantages. The first will allow more familiarity with national systems and, theoretically, more control in consequence, but co-ordination will be difficult. The second throws upon the contractor or consortium the responsibility for sorting out national differences over pricing, delivery arrangements, liabilities and design rights.

As to the protection of design rights, it is often quoted as an advantage of collaboration that it facilitates the transfer of technological know-how between participating countries and their industries, and that this can be especially helpful for smaller nations which might find it difficult to keep up with their competitors in any other way. In practice, each MOU must pay careful attention to principles worked out within NATO for the safeguarding of intellectual property rights (IPR): through membership of NATO, there is an awareness among governments of how each member country can impose secrecy for patented defence inventions and of national practices for proprietary rights. Equally, however, the principles and guidelines applying to the *use* of intellectual property in collaborative projects have been agreed in NATO and widely publicised. The MOD have a high-level agreement with the defence industry to consult before information is exchanged during collaboration, and this has obvious importance in areas where Britain has a technological lead.

Support and Sales

Countries of Western Europe have come to realise in the past decade that maintenance costs form a major part of their procurement budgets. Although the costing of the collaborative projects of the 1960s paid little attention to support aspects of equipment, the current importance attached to life-cycle costing ensures that these aspects are now part of the early discussions on an operational requirement. As much care will now be taken in drafting for the MOU the arrangements to be agreed for co-ordinating support policies as for the management structure itself. As logistics remain a national responsibility within NATO, different supply philosophies have to be taken into account in devising whatever level of integrated support arrangements for the project can be negotiated, covering plans for spare parts, repairs, publication and the control of changes, as well as routine overhaul and maintenance.

Finally, those drafting an MOU will habitually devote special attention to security and sales policy: such policies may initially be in conflict, and a project manager will be well advised to ensure that his negotiating position safeguards both national security and sales interests and, if there is a risk that a partner's diverging sales policy will affect the collaborative programme, to press for joint supervisory arrangements to try to ensure an agreed exports policy. The task will be especially difficult if a partner has a reputation – as, in the past, had France – for giving export requirements a higher priority than military in-service dates.

PARTNERS

With so many and such complex preliminaries to the preparation of an MOU, it is tempting to generalise that the fewer the participating nations, the greater the likelihood of reaching quick agreement and of obtaining the required equipment on time, at the standard and specification needed, and at a cost which would be justified in comparison with national costs, taking account of savings at the expensive development stage. The trend shown by the list in SDE 87 of collaborative projects in which Britain is involved, however, is moving in the direction of more and more participants. The eighteen projects shown as in production or in service (that is, those dating broadly from the 1960s and early 1970s) are divided thus:

Two countries :   9
Three countries : 7 (this would be 8 if SP70 were included)
Five countries :   2

For the nineteen projects which are shown as in development or in earlier study phases (that is, those dating from the late 1970s and early 1980s) the breakdown is:

Two countries :   3
Three countries :   7
Four or more countries : 9[*]

[*]Four of these involve seven or more participants.

Western European countries here seem to face a dilemma. On the one hand, there can be no certainty that a group of more than three or four countries will work together quickly and efficiently enough to produce the benefits sketched out above. On the other hand, CNAD philosophy (as embodied in *NATO Facts and Figures*) included 'the prospect of an enhanced role in defence equipment co-operation for the smaller and less industrialised nations of the Alliance, whose special needs in this area have been increasingly recognised.'[3] This approach is strongly supported in the report by an independent European Defence Industry Study Team to the IEPG in 1987.[4] 'We are convinced that assistance should be given by the other nations of Europe to the efforts of the less developed defence industry (LDDI) nations to strengthen their technological bases and to develop their defence industrial capabilities.' Increasingly, LDDI nations may take on important subcontracting roles in collaborative projects.

With the wide range of products which the defence armoury contains, there need be no contradiction between the need for Britain to ensure that British forces are equipped on time, using collaborative processes wherever possible, and the parallel pressure to join larger collaborative ventures where time-scales are even more liable to slip, costs to escalate and control to be extremely difficult: this will especially be the case when these larger ventures are supported by Nunn–Roth–Warner Amendment funding. Nevertheless experience has shown that comparable problems have not been adequately solved in national programmes. Options for stocking the future armoury are becoming more numerous by the year, and currently can be summarised thus:

(a) develop and purchase nationally;
(b) purchase abroad, developed or off-the-shelf, perhaps as part of a reciprocal arrangement;
(c) collaborate *ab initio* with one or two partners;
(d) collaborate *ab initio* with several partners;
(e) collaborate in development and/or production with one or two partners;
(f) collaborate in development and/or production with several partners.

It will require long and careful study, and often ministerial decisions, before conclusions can be reached as to whether for particular projects the priority is to be the requirement of the British military or the requirement of NATO Europe as a whole.

PEOPLE

Apart from the stresses for governments deriving from the increased complexity and sensitivity of collaborative programmes, new demands are being made of the key individuals in government and industry who will be responsible for the success of future projects through leadership or membership of project teams. In Britain, it is fair to argue that industry is better placed than the public sector to cope with these demands. Through its closer connection with the initial stages of collaborative programmes, industry can now identify far more easily the opportunities upon which particular firms can seize, and thus allocate individuals with known reputations or of particular promise, who will do all possible in their company's interest for the success of the enterprise and who have the prospect of personal advantage (through the flexibility of private sector salary practices) to encourage them to stay with the project. Added to this, many of the major UK-based defence contractors have acquired a 'board-level downwards' familiarity with international work, and know that, under current policies,[5] they 'bear the full responsibility for the successful completion of their contracts,' and 'carrying risk, should have the opportunity for reward if they are successful and efficient in delivering to time, cost and specification.' With the first instruments of European company law which came into effect through the European Economic Community in July 1989, a young manager in a defence-orientated company can be assured of a promising future through association with successful collaborative European projects, taking into account the good success rate to date of such projects.

The prospects for the Crown servant posted to a collaborative project are not as rosy. Publicity tends to centre on those who are involved with the finished product – for example, the photograph on page 46 of SDE 87 of British, German and Italian pilots and navigators training together on the Tornado aircraft. Such operators take up a minor percentage of the military who are involved in collaborative programmes from the conceptual stage. In particular, about one-third of public sector project managers are military, faced with a relatively short posting into the Procurement Executive, not always with the advantage of earlier collaborative work, often confronted with a project which they had no hand in initiating, and likely to move to a next posting with no relevance to project management. Their MOD (PE) posting will be to the appropriate Systems Controllerate (see organisation in Figure 9.1), where lies the policy and day-to-day responsibility for procuring equipment for land, sea and air systems. It will often be a first posting to MOD, and frequently without training specific to the responsibilities to be assumed.

Their civilian counterparts are not necessarily better placed. In fact it is more probable that the military project officer (through his career background and early training) will have better familiarity with the language and culture of the partner country or countries. In 1987, a typical civilian project manager for a major collaborative

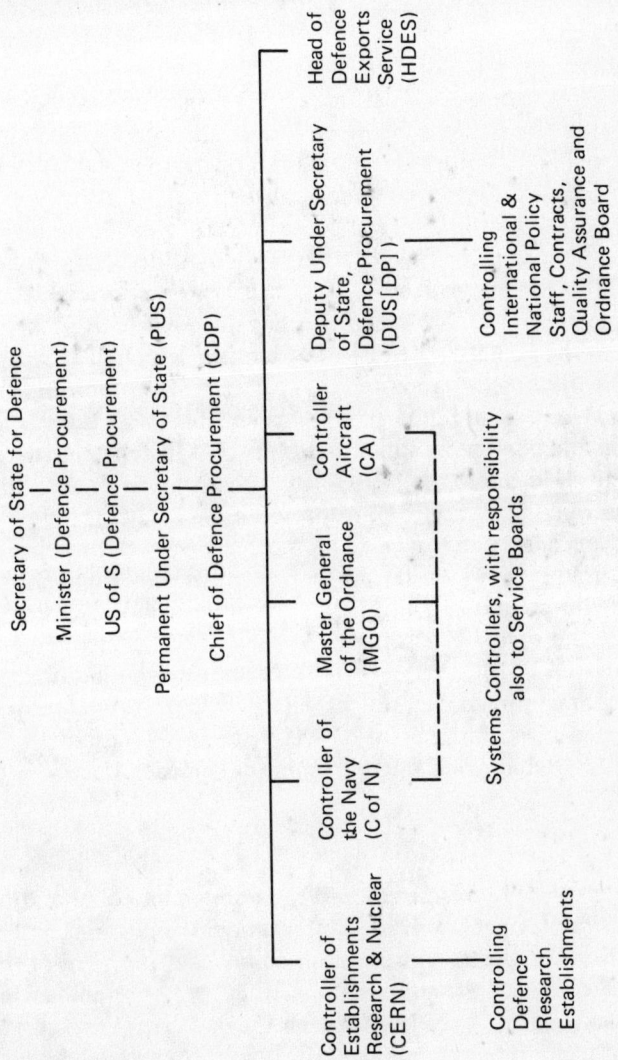

97

Secretary of State for Defence

Minister (Defence Procurement)

US of S (Defence Procurement)

Permanent Under Secretary of State (PUS)

Chief of Defence Procurement (CDP)

| Controller of Establishments Research & Nuclear (CERN) | Controller of the Navy (C of N) | Master General of the Ordnance (MGO) | Controller Aircraft (CA) | Deputy Under Secretary of State, Defence Procurement (DUS[DP]) | Head of Defence Exports Service (HDES) |

Controlling Defence Research Establishments

Systems Controllers, with responsibility also to Service Boards

Controlling International & National Policy Staff, Contracts, Quality Assurance and Ordnance Board

FIGURE 9.1

project will be an engineer, a civil servant with the 'field' responsibility for negotiation with the British firm identified as prime contractor as well as for international negotiations: he will normally report to a Project Director at one-star level working in the relevant Systems Controllerate of the PE, who will be either a military officer or a fellow engineer. Historically, since the Second World War MOD engineers have not fared as well in career terms as their scientific colleagues: after the influence exercised through scientific advice by Lord Zuckerman in the postwar MOD until he moved away in 1966, career MOD scientists have filled several high-level Ministry posts; for example, Sir Clifford Cornford became CDP in 1977, as did Sir David Perry (later CDEC) in 1982. Yet, although Mr Sidney Bacon (Managing Director of the Royal Ordnance Factories from 1972 to 1979) was knighted in 1977, no engineer has since reached a position comparable to the heights scaled by the scientists. Mr Donald Spiers, a senior scientist, was appointed as Controller, Establishments Research and Nuclear, in January 1987, responsible to Mr Levene for the operation and administration of the Ministry's Defence Research Establishments. He is also the head of the new Defence Engineering Service (described in SDE 87), representing the 14 000 civilian engineering specialists, and overseeing a fast-stream career path for high-calibre graduates which began in September 1987: one of the aims behind the creation of the new service is to improve status, opportunities and career prospects.

There has been in MOD a belated realisation of the key role of engineers (military or civilian) in projects, including collaborative projects. Their duties in the latter were succinctly described by Levene to the Public Accounts Committee in March 1986,[6] as consulting

the concept staff, the resources and the equipment collaboration people before they get involved in international discussions and as the discussions progress, so that they can be kept informed of the wider implications of the project upon which they are embarking and of lessons which have been learned on other projects in the past. They have detailed guidance on how to negotiate, how to manage collaborative projects, and we are trying to update this as we go along, because obviously we are getting more experienced in this as the number of collaborative projects grows. The Department also runs training courses[7] to bring staff up-to-date on the negotiation and management of collaborative projects.

Although an engineer (and, more and more, a scientist) has a career background relevant to leading projects in this way, no theoretical reason exists to show why administrators should not be project managers if appropriate technological specialisations are represented within the project team. The Ministry's policy is to integrate contracts staff with project management teams, so as to put the contract function 'at the heart of project management, without division of management authority.'[8] As, additionally to Mr Levene's description of their jobs, project managers must act as the focus for negotiation with the private sector, establishing the causes of any increased costs or delays, taking corrective action and applying necessary pressures on the contractor, the presence of a contracts representative will be an enormous help to them. Indeed, it can be visualised that contracts staff would themselves be well placed to be project managers were it not that the increased load placed upon the function as a result of competition policies must make it difficult to select and train appropriate individuals. The National Audit Office (NAO), in a long report, in July 1986, on the MOD's control and management of the development of major equipment, made ominous noises to the effect that project management often suffered from staffing constraints and that staffing difficulties of this nature would inevitably reduce MOD's ability to detect problems at an early enough stage for remedial action.[9] The decisions taken to move first the Royal Ordnance Factories and, more recently, the Defence Research Establishments out of the public sector compound the Ministry's problem of identifying project managers.

The NAO report was generally critical of the Ministry's failure to overcome problems of cost escalation and delays affecting major projects. In the collaborative field, an earlier report by Parliament's Defence Committee had commented that industry 'sees considerable scope for improving on current management arrangements.'[10] It is thus comforting to record, that, in its 1984/5 report on ten collaborative projects, the Public Accounts Committee noted that 'the Comptroller and Auditor General concluded that, having regard to the inherent limitations, MOD had been largely successful in seeking to exercise a high level of control and management over the collaborative projects he examined:[11] the administrative improvements outlined above have been implemented since that report, and the British management position for negotiating with potential collaborative partners should be strengthened in proportion.

A factor not identified by the PAC in this comment, and which has been an obstacle up to now for the MOD project manager, has been the delay resulting from the hierarchical ministry through which he receives policy instructions. Although much has been done (in line with the policy just outlined) to give increased responsibility and expert staff to project managers, an MOD management report, *Learning from Experience*[12] indicated in 1987 that projects costing more than £13 million to develop and £25 million to produce must pass through six layers of bureaucratic reviews; the report referred to widespread frustration among project managers at delays and remoteness from major decisions, in stark contrast to the practice in industry; also to a reluctance to learn from past histories, when such histories were available, to the extent that the *Compendium of Guidelines for Project Managers* published by the Ministry does not in fact tell project managers how their tasks should be performed. The point on layers of bureaucratic reviews was illustrated by the organisation diagram (Figure 9.2) together with a radical proposal for a rationalised hierarchy.

If the report's comments reflect accurately the prevailing situation, the points made are of the greatest importance to the equipment collaborative future, challenging the comfortable findings of the PAC as recorded above. The position of the MOD project manager in relation to his industrial colleagues and collaborative partners is worse than the PAC imagined, as are the control processes of the Ministry. On the other hand, the proposed new decisions-making chain in Figure 9.2 involves managers of one project reporting direct to four-star Systems Controllers and, remembering the large number of major projects at various stages for which the MOD are responsible, this would place an even heavier load on the top-level posts. So, despite the advantages of submerging the collaborative responsibility in MOD within the Procurement Executive outlined in Chapter 5, the final question of this long chapter to the reader may well be whether the Rayner and Heseltine reforms, radical as they were, have gone far enough to match Britain's organisation for collaboration with those of our collaborative partners in terms of efficient and speedy decision making.

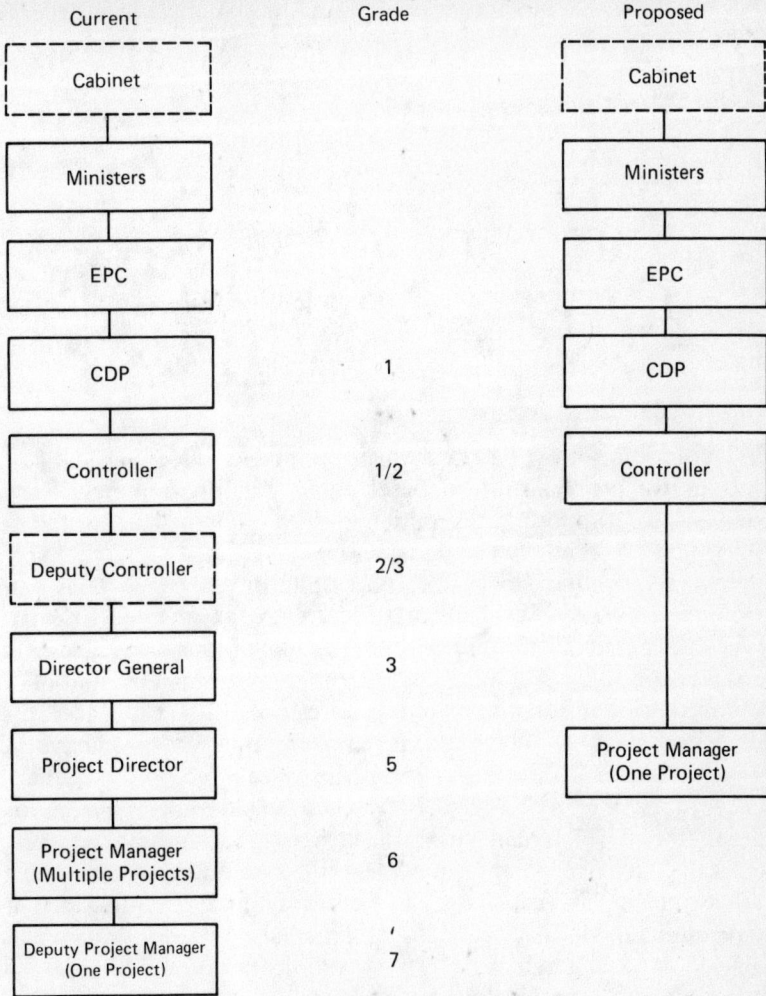

Current	Grade	Proposed
Cabinet		Cabinet
Ministers		Ministers
EPC		EPC
CDP	1	CDP
Controller	1/2	Controller
Deputy Controller	2/3	
Director General	3	
Project Director	5	Project Manager (One Project)
Project Manager (Multiple Projects)	6	
Deputy Project Manager (One Project)	7	

FIGURE 9.2

10 British Policy Towards Equipment Collaboration: A Summary and a Forward Look

Collaboration is not a panacea which will magically cure all the cost and control problems which beset equipment programmes. Each collaborative proposal will continue to be examined against cost benefit criteria and, when decisions to proceed are taken, likely success will continue to depend on careful drafting of MOUs and strong appropriate management structures being manned by high-class government and industry staff. These conditions themselves will depend on a successful matching of military requirements and on a readiness to compromise in the interest of all. These are stiff conditions to meet, but have the major armaments producers in Western Europe, and the Defence Ministries which provide them with orders, any real choice other than collaboration (before or during the development stage) against the background of ever-increasing defence equipment costs and of defence budgets which shrink annually in real terms? The disadvantages of co-production were outlined in Chapter 1. As to national ventures, the French decision to build a fighter aircraft unilaterally has brought enormous difficulty, with high development and production costs meaning that huge sales abroad will be needed – but in competition with the modernised F16 and the EFA. In this final chapter, it will be convenient to end by taking each of the three main headings used in this book (NATO, the defence industry and the Ministry of Defence) and summarising the present position and the outlook for the 1990s.

NATO

As explained in Chapter 4, NATO's responsibility for armaments co-operation between member countries has been greatly aided in the last four years by the enhanced authority given to the CNADs and the IEPG, and by the working programmes set in motion by both these groups. Inevitably, small cracks are appearing in the organisational structures and programmes set up since 1985 – progress on some of the twelve working programmes identified by the CNADs by April 1987 has already been delayed because some nations have failed to produce funds, or have decided to withdraw from projects in which they had expressed an interest. This will continue to be one of the hazards of collaboration, for which no answer is immediately available within what Dr Luns has described as NATO's 'balance of mutual benefits and responsibilities:'[1] to seek financial guarantees before nations joined collaborative study groups would be to impose an artificial constraint on the process. Up to 1984, it was reasonable to think of collaboration in the words of the familiar Johnsonian quotation: 'It is not well done, but you are surprised to find it done at all.' With all the improvements in approach and procedures which have been achieved in the last four years, it is now safe to claim that, if it is not well done before the end of this century, it will be because national considerations and prejudices in Europe have finally outweighed the benefits (military, political and industrial) to be obtained.

A fundamental dilemma remains, that at a time when the US Administration has bestowed great favour and help upon inter-European collaboration and increased US purchases from Europe, American industry will naturally do all possible to capture European markets and to spoil European efforts to unify a defence industry. Equally, the US Administration will be keen to see success with the trans-Atlantic collaborative markets. Finally, despite the uncertainty and frustrations of the US procurement system, major British defence firms, for example BAe, have an important reliance on American and Canadian sales. So a crucial balancing act must be performed in years to come by the CNAD (under American chairmansip into the foreseeable future, and with a NATO international secretariat) and the IEPG (under European chairmanship) in ensuring a division of the development of future projects between European countries alone and European countries linked with the United States, such as will ensure orders, employment and markets as a priority for European firms. In recent years the arms market has become the target of competition from unexpected areas, for example, Brazil. The 1947 Japanese Constitution, in renouncing war, prohibited Japanese manufacture of offensive weapons, but there has been a steady increase in the use of Japanese dual-use projects in American systems; and the partnerships between Kawasaki and MBB for the BK117 helicopter, and between Alfa Romeo and Nissan for a dual-use light 4x4 vehicle, could be unfavourable omens for inter-European collaboration. The IEPG is well placed to decide projects which should be moved towards European collaboration and those which should be earmarked for co-operation with the United States.

To aid the IEPG in this task, there is a strong case for the governments of the four European countries with the longest history and experience in collaborative work (the United Kingdom, France, the FRG and Italy) deciding upon bilateral or trilateral arrangements for developing those common requirements which the IEPG identifies, through a series of inter-governmental meetings with military and industrial representatives present. It cannot be too strongly emphasised that a priority for the military is to obtain equipment in good time, as delay increases the risk of built-in obsolescence. The IEPG is valuable but to wait until all countries involved have had time to consider their future programme plans (and for less developed countries this is obviously more difficult than for the others) is to pay a price in terms of time which can easily outweigh other potential advantages. A clear starting-point for the United Kingdom is to seek as much partnership as possible with France. The foundation stone for close co-operation in armaments procurement was laid at a meeting between Mr Younger and M. Giraud, his French counterpart in mid-March 1987, when agreement in principle was reached to review mutual defence requirements and identify contract opportunities for each country's defence industries. As Sir Nicholas Henderson pointed out in a recent work,[2] the French look after their own interests 'with exceptional skill and assiduity', and the views of their leaders about Britain 'are apt to oscillate between rivalry and contempt'. Nevertheless, the overall Anglo-French record of collaboration in military projects is good, many French military interests and historic commitments coincide with those of Britain, there are recent signs of a French desire to edge closer to NATO – and there is a fair risk that, given Franco-German military co-operation in the last decade, if Britain does not look for closer equipment collaboration with France, the FRG authorities will! It could be productive if the series of inter-governmental meetings suggested were to begin with France, and be followed by comparable meetings with the FRG and Italy, enabling the four countries to come to the IEPG with well-developed agreements for development, which other countries could join at later stages. This would repeat the early NATO experience, whereby, rather than await the results of interminable all-country meetings (and a family saying in NATO circles is that 'the convoy moves at the speed of its slowest ship'!), bilateral or trilateral plans were presented as *faits accomplis* to committees involved in armaments co-operation. The main advantage of this approach would be to build up for the next century strong Western European defence industry links such as could be the basis for effective competition with the United States. An alternative would be for France and Britain to be partners in rivalry with the FRG and Italy, bringing the advantage of competition within Western Europe. Such groupings might seem, at least initially, disadvantageous to the smaller European members of NATO, but, as time went by, their skills and manpower might be attached to one or other grouping as a result of inter-governmental negotiation.

Such inter-governmental meetings could profitably research two main potential fields of collaboration. The need to reduce high development costs is normally quoted as a major reason for initiating a collaborative project. A logical first step for Britain and France to take, against the background of future IEPG work, is to compare current and future development programmes and, where there is duplication or where broadly similar programmes have been approved, to take action to merge programmes or, failing this, to agree to abandon one programme in favour of the other, in readiness for a joint approach to market that programme within the IEPG. Although a logical approach, such comparison of development programmes has rarely taken place (except on an *ad hoc* basis) over the thirty years of collaborative history. The mould was broken by the first bilateral conference of governmental and industrial experts to extend reciprocal purchases, held in Lancaster House on 17 and 18 September 1987, when, according to a report in *The Times* on 19 September, certain army weapons systems (being developed by one or other of the participators) were identified in the planned armouries which might be reciprocally purchased to reduce national development costs. This was reportedly seen by the French as an important step towards a European common market in arms; as, however, it was not until 1988 that naval and air procurement plans are compared, and as no positive statements were made after the conference on the timing of approaches to other Western European arms producers, there must be a probability that no such common market will be established in the present century.

The second field of collaboration would be *ab initio*; military and industrial representatives of the two nations would look together at IEPG requirements with the aim of producing a combined bid adequate to obtain IEPG approval that it would be in the general interest of Western European nations for work to be left to the two countries up to at least the development stage, rather than for delays to be built in by the addition of other collaborative partners in the early stages. Dr Hartley's contention that, if two equal partners combine their national orders, each will save at least 35 per cent on R&D, and up to 10 per cent on production costs,[3] has not yet been disproved, and should hold out to other IEPG members the likelihood of worthwhile savings on their equipment programmes of delegating bilaterally in this way. There are enough examples already to hand of what is likely to happen within Europe if this approach is *not* followed for collaborative projects. For example, the NATO plan for collaboration on a seven-nation basis on a long-foreseen CNAD requirement for short-range and long-range stand-off missiles (which was approved in Rome in November 1986) is steadily drifting into the sands because of the difficulty of getting seven nations to think along the same lines; the consequence, realistically, can be seen as being that national or bilateral developments to meet these requirements will be favoured by national military authorities and will continue in parallel with, and more quickly than, the wider development, just because national military leaders, reasonably enough, cannot accept the delays which multi-partnerships involve.

After exploration of the possibilities within these two approaches with the French, the same procedure would be followed with the Germans and Italians. It might be tempting for governments to concentrate on one of these approaches to the detriment of the other and, in terms of cost-saving and immediate value for money, the preferred course would probably be to aim to fill national armouries with items which have been, or are about to be, developed, dividing the programme on a specialised basis between the four countries. This option is arguably less favourable to Britain's long-term interests: for many years Britain has led her continental neighbours in terms of the effort devoted to defence R&D, enabling engineers and scientists in government and defence firms to build up significant in-house and industrial expertise and skill in the design of systems. Apart from contributing directly to defence programmes, this provided a facility for intelligent criticism of defence contractors' proposals which made the MOD an informed customer. To an extent this capability will be eroded through the planned move into the private sector of MOD's Defence Research Establishments, although in national terms the balance *vis-à-vis* the continent has remained in Britain's favour. To retain this advantage, as well as a national capability for design as a keystone for collaboration, it will be necessary for enough priority projects to be led by Britain to enable the R&D facility to be kept at its maximum, and, for this, MOD would have to insist on an appropriate balance being maintained between *ab initio* development (which retains the R&D effort) and specialisation (which distributes the effort throughout Europe).

Evidently there are significant political difficulties in this bilateral approach to future collaboration, which logically would be as appropriate to the CNAD organisation as to the IEPG. A major problem is the political obligation on advanced NATO countries to bring along the less developed defence industries in the wake of the more developed, so as to strengthen the Alliance as a whole. However well-meaning NATO governments show themselves towards this philosophy, defence industries themselves will see no obligation to give altruistic help where there are obviously no profits to be gained from aiding slower partners. Although the IEPG are currently grappling with this problem, an alternative approach would be to transfer it to American leadership under the CNAD organisation, leaving European collaboration *ab initio* to be fostered under bilateral arrangements, with production (and in some cases development) seen as the area in which the input and skills of the less developed defence industries could be more appropriately used. There was, however, no indication in the communiqué issued after the June 1987 meeting that IEPG ministers were prepared to relinquish their efforts to make progress in this delicate area. All member countries were urged to help to develop the industries of the LDDI countries, to encourage their participation in joint ventures, to give them access to the latest defence technology and to allow LDDI industries to compete more successfully in the other nations' procurement projects and in collaborative programmes. Simultaneously, a note of cautionary prudence for the LDDI countries was struck in the emphasis that their defence spending should be balanced against the returns they receive. These objectives as seen as long-term, and the reactions of defence companies in the more advanced NATO countries, and indeed of the LDDI countries themselves (perhaps, as already suggested in Chapter 9, in a subcontracting role), will form an interesting background to the development of Western Europe itself in the last decade of the century.

THE BRITISH DEFENCE INDUSTRY

Chapter 6 suggests that major British defence firms have made tremendous strides in the last decade in the direction of improved collaboration and competition with major Western European firms. A recent *Flight International* editorial suggest, in the context of the BAe/Rover deal, that 'ossified industrial structures, with single-sector companies serving single-country markets, have no place in modern international markets',[4] and this philosophy must surely be shared by MOD (PE) in so far as it accepts any planning responsibility for the industry's future in the next decade, although MOD statements on how they see this are conspicuous by their absence. It was already clear at the time of the Plowden Report in 1965 that Britain could never afford again to embark on her own on a major aerospace project, and the same has applied for some time to major defence projects in other military areas. The expert judgement of *Flight International* is that Europe's electronic industries have made commendable efforts in recent years to catch up with American and Japanese technologies, but that governments should abandon their view that, in multinational projects, competition should be excluded through insistence that national industries should have a share of the work.[5] This is an interesting concept, with application beyond the electronics field, but a more important first stage, as Sir Frank Cooper urged in 1986 is for Europe to achieve a more coherent defence industrial base, which he saw as crucial to the future cohesiveness of Europe within the Western Alliance.[6]

For the defence industry, the European collaborative future must lie in seeking more teaming arrangements within the United Kingdom and with companies in Western Europe, whether these be traditional partners or erstwhile competitors. Just as a collaborative project represents to the British military one that is less liable to be cancelled, because of the involvement of other countries, so the defence industry – faced with a long history of government cancellations and indecision – must view collaborative projects, with all their difficulties, as offering less risk of cancellation or postponement than national projects. Equally in export markets there should be a better chance of success and an improved ability to compete with the US defence industry. Within the defence industry certain sectors (especially those connected with the construction of aircraft missiles, land vehicles and warships) will remain more dependent on defence orders for their survival than others (for example, electronics and information technology firms). In France, the FRG and Italy, much of the same applies, although particular firms in all four countries will have protected their futures by diversification into production for the civil sector. The EEC is currently aiming to increase the creation of big European companies and joint ventures. Sometimes the British government has actively intervened with measures which seem to have been aimed at aiding this objective and encouraging a resistance to take-over by American firms (as with Ford/Austin Rover); sometimes, the policy seems to have taken an opposite tack, as with Westland/Sikorsky and the withdrawal from the NH90 project. Within Britain, major defence firms look from time to time at the possibility of take-over, and the MOD will inevitably be interested in any such developments for the sake of keeping down the cost of defence contracts through discouraging monopolies – witness the strong MOD opposition before the Monopolies Commission to GEC's attempt to take over Plessey in 1985. There is, however, a balancing act to be accomplished if British companies are to continue to team successfully with continental countries in bidding for defence contracts with the aim of competing effectively with American firms; it will be necessary for British firms to retain adequate size and resources to match those continental firms with which they are to be associated. It is feasible that, in the last decade of the century, the British government will be faced with bids from continental defence interests to take over British firms, and difficult balances will need to be struck in terms of the implications for Britain's future resources, markets and employment prospects.

As a result of policies, governmental and internal, which have been applied in the 1980s, Britain's defence firms appear well placed to meet these challenges. Above all, they have a supply of high-calibre project managers, well capable of matching their continental opposite numbers as a result of their previous collaborative experience and of the status and authority given to them within their organisations. The standardisation resulting from a European free market in

1992 will make management easier, as will the opening of the Channel Tunnel. The confidence of British firms under present conditions is well illustrated by the increasing number of private ventures being initiated, often in collaboration with European firms, in the expectation of attracting support from West European defence ministries.

THE MINISTRY OF DEFENCE

It can be confidently stated that MOD has had, and will continue to have, the greatest problems of all over equipment collaboration – not so much at the political level, where successive Secretaries of State and Ministers of State have made all the right and necessary statements: the ministerial responsibility must be mainly to assert political will at all the critical stages of major projects, as the success of an international project contributes significantly to national pride, although failure (as with the SP70) can lead to considerable political embarrassment. The major executive problems occur for those military and civilian authorities who identify potential collaborative projects, who are concerned with the preparation of MOUs and contracts, and who ultimately undertake the project management. On identification, options are becoming narrower almost each year: independent production of a major project (defining 'major' for the purpose according to the planned spending levels for which ministeral authorisation is required, that is, £13 million for development and £25 million for production) will rarely be possible, and foreign purchase is beset with problems of its own. To buy from a country which subsidises its defence contractors will attract howls of rage at a time when government policy is to remove subsidies from British industry. At a time when the MOD proclaims (SDE 87, paragraph 506) that the responsibility for supplying defence equipment of the specified quality rests with the contractor, there must be suspicion that what appears to be gained in terms of price and costs in a foreign purchase may well be through less compliance with quality standards than would be expected of a British firm, and the British military have less control over design and specifications. Offset arrangements, although superficially attractive in the overall national interest, may turn out to be less favourable when balanced against these considera-tions. Yet, if the Ministry has inadequate funds available for research and development, foreign purchase may be the only option available.

The moving of the Defence Research Establishments away from government control will present its own difficulties to those with the responsibility for initiating projects, because it will move a source of instant technological advice and of potential project managers into the private sector, although the staff involved in the move may find benefits in terms of pay and conditions and be available for secondment to MOD project teams. The hope must be that, if operational requirements staff are given more control over research budgets as a result of the change, they will be able in consequence to exercise more choice and value for money in relation to the work of the Establishments. All this would then form part of a move towards improving the management of defence projects.

Yet it is in project management itself that the greatest problems can be predicted. Project management began to be identified as a skill only in the 1970s. When Mr Peter Levene joined the MOD, no central list of project managers was held, and little correlation was made between their training and their careers. Their responsibilities were submerged in a hierarchy of management of which they were the lowest professional rung: for those responsible for more than one project, these problems were multiplied. There is no obvious homogeneity between service and civilian project managers, who follow their separate recruitment and careers. The 'hands-off' policy with defence contractors described in Chapter 6 has the implication that a project manager, although given the direct interface with his industrial counterparts and a professional supporting team, is more concerned with monitoring a project than with managing it – yet, if something goes wrong, it will be the MOD representatives who are called to account by Parliament and not the contractor. So it is fair to conclude that, although Levene has done a great deal to improve the status and authority of project managers, much remains which could be done in terms of providing the project manager with objectives, resources and the authority to trade time, cost, capacity and risk when project work so demands. The Jordan–Lee–Cawsey report, mentioned in Chapter 9, drew attention to reforms needed to enhance the status of the project manager, and may prove a turning-point for further improvements.

As a final summary, it has to be accepted that there will inevitably be continuing discussion of the advantages and disadvantages of collaboration at many political and military levels in the decade ahead. Some critics will be pessimistic about their outcome, and argue that national self-interest and commercial gain will always be more powerful motivators than the complex procedures involved in collaboration. Yet, looking back over the last thirty years, it is impossible to end this survey on a pessimistic note. So much was achieved between 1984 and 1987 in both the CNAD and IEPG areas in moving away from *ad hoc* ventures towards a coherent and balanced approach to collaboration that it is not realistic to imagine that these efforts represent only a transitional phase, and that NATO nations will drift back into national incoherence. Both the NATO organisation itself and its major participating member states are now so committed as to make it reasonable to forecast that, in ten years' time, failure to collaborate successfully in major weapons systems' development will be seen as intolerable. The military and political consequences for the Alliance itself of such a positive approach will be proportionately advantageous.

Notes

1 STAGES FOR COLLABORATION

1. 'Major' may usefully be defined in financial terms applied by the Ministry of Defence in categorising projects in 1987, as projects estimated to cost over £50 million for development or over £100 million for production.

2. Egon Klepsch, *Two Way Street* (London: Brassey's, 1979).

2 THE NATO BACKGROUND: 1957 TO 1976

1. DEFE 7, 1950.

2. *NATO Facts and Figures 1989*, p.177.

3. D. W. Urwin, *Western Europe Since 1945* (London: Longman, 1968).

4. A. Sampson, *Anatomy of Britain* (London: Hodder & Stoughton, 1962).

5. *RAF Quarterly*, vol. 11, no. 2, Summer 1962.

6. *Le Monde*, 1 December 1965.

7. *NATO Facts and Figures 1981*, p. 162

8. *NATO Facts and Figures 1981*, p. 165

9. *Statement on the Defence Estimates (SDE) 1966*, Part I, III, paragraph 8.

10. *SDE 1966*, Part I, III, paragraph 12.

11. The Joint Staff Requirement was issued in September 1964 and the Anglo-French Memorandum of Understanding was signed, and contracts placed, during 1965.

12. *SDE 1966,* Part II, IV, paragraph 21.

13. Plowden Report, Cmnd 2863 (London: HMSO, 1965).

14. T. Callaghan, *NATO – The Next Thirty Years* (London: Westview/Croom Helm, 1980) p. 305.

15. *Towards a Stronger Europe,* report of the IEPG's European Defence Industry Study Team, 1987.

16. A. Grosser, *The Western Alliance* (London: Macmillan, 1978); J.-J. Servan-Schreiber, *The American Challenge* (New York: Athenaeum, 1979); F. A. Beer, *Integration and Disintegration in NATO* (Ohio State University Press, 1969).

17. A. Reed, *Britain's Aircraft Industry* (London: J. M.Dent,1973).

18. The only major new collaborative projects for which joint development was initiated in the 1970s and early 1980s were the Sea Gnat project to develop decoy systems, the NATO frigate and the ill-fated SP70.

3 MINISTRY OF DEFENCE ORGANISATION AND COLLABORATION: 1957 TO 1976

1. Cmnd 4641 (London: HMSO, April 1971).

2. Ministry of Defence Organisation and Procurement, June 1982.

3. Cmnd 4641 (London: HMSO, April 1971) paragraph 17.

4. Cmnd 2853 (London: HMSO, December 1965) Annex M.

5. *Defence in the 1980s,* Cmnd 7826 (London: HMSO) paragraph 737.

6. House of Commons Defence Committee, 2nd Report Session 1981/2, paragraph 1.

7. House of Commons Defence Committee, 2nd Report Session 1981/2, paragraphs 59 & 60.

4 THE NATO BACKGROUND: 1976 TO 1987

1. D. W. Urwin, *Western Europe Since 1945* (London: Longman, 1968).

2. General Bernard W. Rogers, 'Western Europe Security and European Defence', *RUSI Journal,* vol. 131, no. 3, September 1986, p. 11.

3. *Jane's Defence Weekly,* 11 April 1987.

4. Jan van Houwelingen, 'The IEPG – The Way Ahead', *NATO Review,* 4 August 1984.

5. *SDE 1985,* paragraph 321.

6. William Taft, 'NATO defence co-operation: a new era', *Jane's Defence Weekly,* 8 August 1987.

7. European Fighters for the Next Century, *RUSI Newsbrief,* February 1986.

8. *The Times,* 17 March 1988.

9. *Financial Times,* 8 March 1988.

5 MINISTRY OF DEFENCE ORGANISATION AND COLLABORATION: 1976 TO 1987

1. House of Commons Defence Committee, 2nd Report, June 1982.

2. House of Commons Defence Committee, 2nd Report, June 1982, paragraph 10.

3. Geoffrey Pattie, *Value for Money,* Defence Open Government, 83/01.

6   THE DEFENCE INDUSTRY AND COLLABORATION: 1957 TO 1987

1. The Defence Sales Organisation was established in 1966, as a result of recommendations from Lord Stokes to Mr Denis Healey.

2. F. A. Beer, *Integration and Disintegration in NATO* (Ohio State University Press, 1969).

3. N. Ball and M. Leitenburg, *The Structure of the Defence Industry* (London: Croom Helm, 1983).

4. A. Reed, *Britain's Aircraft Industry* (London: J. M. Dent, 1973).

5. 'European Collaboration and the British Government', *International Affairs* vol. 63, no. 1.

6. Defence Open Government Document 83/01, paragraph 1 of Annex A.

7. *SDE* 1980, paragraph 736.

8. Defence Open Government Document 83/01, paragraph 8.

9. Evidence printed in Sixth Report Session 1986/7, 'Control and Management of the Development of Major Equipment'.

7. THE ROYAL NAVY AND COLLABORATION

1. Paragraph 2413 of evidence on the 35th Report from the Public Accounts Committee (HC 452), 14 May 1986.

2. *Independent*, 6 October 1987.

3. The Rt Hon. Lord Prior comments in *A Balance of Power* (London: Hamish Hamilton, 1986) that, 'although it is loss-making, Harland and Wolff is an essential part of the economy of Northern Ireland, not just for the jobs and skill it provides, not only for the sub-contractors who get their living from the yards, but also because of its symbolic importance'.

4. Public Accounts Committee, 31st Report, published 1988.

5. Defence Committee, 3rd Report Session 1984/5, vol. 1, paragraphs 28 and 29, printed 23 May 1985.

6. *Towards a Stronger Europe*, report of the IEPG European Defence Industry Study Team, vol 2, p. 69.

7. *Towards a Stronger Europe*, report of the IEPG European Defence Industry Study Team, vol 2, pp. 112–23.

8 CASE-STUDIES IN COLLABORATION

1. M. M. Posten, *British War Production* (London: HMSO, 1957); W. Hornby, *Factories and Plant* (London: HMSO, 1958); M. M. Posten, P. Hay and J. D. Scott, *Design and Development of Weapons* (London: HMSO, 1964).

2. The Official War Histories make clear that Vickers Armstrong Ltd were the major wartime producers of British tanks.

3. The decision was to give Vickers plc one year in which to produce an improved Challenger in line with the operational requirement.

4. R. Gardner and R. Longstaff, *British Service Helicopters* (London: Robert Hale, 1985).

5. *The Economist*, 21 June 1986.

6. J. Everett-Heath, *British Military Helicopters* (London: Arms & Armour Press, 1986).

7. Of Aerospatiale's helicopter orders in 1987, 55 per cent came from Europe and 78 per cent of total orders were for export; two-thirds of all orders were for military helicopters.

8. 'European Collaboration and the British Government', *International Affairs,* vol. 63, no. 1

9. Allison Gas Turbines, quoted in *Flight International,* 20 February 1988.

9   PROBLEMS, PARTNERS AND PEOPLE

1. A. Sampson, *The Arms Bazaar* (London: Hodder & Stoughton, 1977).

2. Jane's Defence Weekly, 15 August 1987.

3. *NATO Facts and Figures 1981,* p. 168.

4. *Towards a Stronger Europe,* report of the IEPG European Defence Industry Study Team, vol. 2

5. *SDE 1986,* paragraph 526.

6. Paragraph 12705, Minutes of Evidence, summarised in paragraph 4 of the 35th Report of the Public Accounts Committee, Session 1985/6.

7. For example, the courses at RMCS Shrivenham, which are attended also by defence industry representatives and French and German students.

8. *SDE 1986,* paragraph 526.

9. National Audit Office 568, Part 5, paragraph 5.4

10. House of Commons Defence Committee, 2nd Report, Session 1981/2, paragraph 114.

11. Public Accounts Committee, 5th Report, Session 1984/5, paragraph 8.

12. G. Jordan, I. Lee and G. Cawsey, *Report to the Minister (Defence Procurement)* (London: HMSO, 1988).

10 BRITISH POLICY TOWARDS EQUIPMENT COLLABORATION: A SUMMARY AND A FORWARD LOOK

1. *NATO Facts and Figures 1981*, preface.

2. N. Henderson, *Channels and Tunnels* (London: Weidenfield & Nicolson, 1987).

3. K. Hartley, *NATO Arms Co-operation* (London: Allen & Unwin, 1983).

4. *Flight International*, 12 March 1988.

5. *Flight International*, 19 March 1988.

6. 'The European Pillar in Armament Production', *NATO's Sixteen Nations*, June 1986.

Selected Bibliography

Ball, N. and Leitenberg, M., *The Structure of the Defence Industry* (London: Croom Helm, 1983).

Beer, F. A., *Integration and Disintegration in NATO* (Ohio State University Press, 1969).

Everett-Heath, J., *British Military Helicopters* (London: Arms & Armour Press, 1986).

Gardner, R. and Longstaff, R., *British Service Helicopters* (London: Robert Hale, 1985).

Grosser, A., *The Western Alliance* (London: Macmillan, 1978).

Henderson, N., *Channels and Tunnels* (London: Weidenfeld & Nicolson, 1987).

Hornby, W., *Factories and Plant* (London: HMSO, 1958).

Jordan, G., Lee, I. and Cawsey, G., *Report to The Minister (Defence Procurement)* (London: HMSO, 1988).

Klepsch, E., *Two-Way Street* (Brassey's 1979).

Myers, A., *NATO: The Next 30 Years* (Westview/Croom Helm, 1968).

Postan, M. M., *British War Production* (London: HMSO, 1957).

Postan, M. M., *Design and Development of Weapons* (London: HMSO, 1964).

Prior, J., *A Balance of Power* (London: Hamish Hamilton, 1986).

Reed, A., *Britain's Aircraft Industry* (London: J. M. Dent, 1973).

Sampson, A., *Anatomy of Britain* (London: Hodder & Stoughton, 1962).

Sampson, A., *The Arms Bazaar* (London: Macmillan, 1978).

Servan-Schreiber, J.-J., *The American Challenge* (Athenaeum, 1979).

Servan-Schreiber, J.-J., *NATO Facts and Figures* (NATO 1981).

Urwin, D. W., *Western Europe Since 1947* (London: Longman, 1968).

Plus many articles in Command publications, defence journals, Aldelphi papers and the European Press, some of which are specified in the text.

Country Index

The index has been arranged in two ways: the first lists entries in a country-by-country basis; and the second on a traditional alphabetical basis. The second index starts on page 128.

Weapons and Equipment

Europe

Institutions and Titles

Federal Republic of Germany

Authors and Publications

Spain

Weapons and Equipment

EFA, European Fighter
Aircraft 42, 46, 47, 65, 86,
88, 89, 90, 91, 92, 102
NH90 82, 83, 84, 85, 86, 109

United States of America

Authors and Publications

Callaghan, Thomas 27

Defence Industry

Sikorsky 109

Institutions and Titles

Defense Industry Export Advisory
Group 58
Nunn–Roth–Warner 95

Personalities

Carter, President 27, 28, 39, 41,
43
Eisenhower, President 2, 3, 17, 21

Godwin, R. 33
Kennedy, President John 23
Nixon, President Richard 28, 41
Nunn, Senator Sam 43, 44
Nunn–Roth–Warner 95
Reagan, President Ronald 33
Rogers, General Bernard 42
Taft, Robert 46

Weapons and Equipment

Abrams M-IAI 78
Amraam, Advanced
Medium-Range Anti-Aircraft
Missile 41, 89
Apache 83
ATF, Advanced Tactical
Fighter 42
AWACS, Airborne Warning &
Control System 21, 37
Black Hawk 82, 83, 84, 85
F111 24
F16 102
F18 47
Hawk 9, 18
LHX Helicopter 83
Sidewinder 9, 18
Variable Geometry Project 28

**For other countries, see alphabetical
index**

Alphabetical Index